D0990119

Forensic
Chemistry

Forensic
Chemistry

DAVID E. NEWTON

Facts On File
An imprint of Infobase Publishing

Forensic Chemistry

Facts On File, Inc.
An imprint of Infobase Publishing
132 West 31st Street
New York NY 10001

ISBN-10: 0-8160-5275-1
ISBN-13: 978-0-8160-5275-2

Library of Congress Cataloging-in-Publication Data
Newton, David E.
    Forensic chemistry / David E. Newton.
        p. cm.—(The new chemistry)
    Includes bibliographical references and index.
    ISBN 0-8160-5275-1
1. Chemistry, Forensic. I. Title.
    RA1057.N49 2007
    363.25—dc22   2006034080

Text design by James Scotto-Lavino
Illustrations by DiacriTech, LLC
Project editing by Dorothy Cummings

Printed in the United States of America

MP CGI 10 9 8 7 6 5 4 3 2 1

This book is printed on acid-free paper.

One Last Time . . .
for

John McArdle, Lee Nolet, Richard Olson, David Parr,
David Rowand, Jeff Williams, and John D'Emilio

Thanks for the memories!

◆

CONTENTS

◆ PREFACE

The subject matter covered in introductory chemistry classes at the middle and high school levels tends to be fairly traditional and relatively consistent from school to school. Topics that are typically covered in such classes include atomic theory, chemical periodicity, ionic and covalent compounds, equation writing, stoichiometry, and solutions. While these topics are essential for students planning to continue their studies in chemistry or the other sciences and teachers are correct in emphasizing their importance, they usually provide only a limited introduction to the rich and exciting character of research currently being conducted in the field of chemistry. Many students not planning to continue their studies in chemistry or the other sciences may benefit from information about areas of chemistry with immediate impact on their daily lives or of general intellectual interest. Indeed, science majors themselves may also benefit from the study of such subjects.

The New Chemistry is a set of six books intended to provide an overview of some areas of research not typically included in the middle or high school chemistry curriculum. The six books in the set—*Chemistry of Drugs, Chemistry of New Materials, Forensic Chemistry, Chemistry of the Environment, Food Chemistry,* and *Chemistry of Space*—are designed to provide a broad, general introduction to some fields of chemistry that are less commonly mentioned in standard introductory chemistry courses. They cover topics ranging from the most fundamental fields of chemistry, such as the origins of matter and of the universe, to those with important applications to everyday life, such as the composition of foods and drugs. The set title The New Chemistry has been selected to emphasize the extensive review of recent research and advances in each of the fields of chemistry covered in the set. The books in The New Chemistry set are written for middle school and high school readers. They assume some basic understanding of the principles of chemistry that are generally gained in an introductory middle or high school course in the subject. Every book contains a large amount of material that should be accessible to the interested reader with no more than an introductory understanding of chemistry and a smaller amount of material that may require a more advanced understanding of the subject.

The six books that make up the set are independent of each other. That is, readers may approach all of the books in any sequence whatsoever. To assist the reader in extending his or her understanding of each subject, each book in the set includes a glossary and a list of additional reading sources from both print and Internet sources. Short bibliographic sketches of important figures from each of the six fields are also included in the books.

INTRODUCTION

T he general public's fascination with forensic science is unquestioned. Over the past decade, television programs focusing on the solution of crimes—such as *Law & Order* and *CSI: Crime Scene Investigation* and their spin-offs—have consistently topped popularity charts in the United States and other nations. Viewers seem to be captivated by the crime-solving tools that law enforcement officers have at their disposal and the skills with which they use those tools. The appeal of crime stories is not new. Going back at least as far as Edgar Allan Poe's "The Murder in the Rue Morgue" (1841) and Wilkie Collins's *The Woman in White* (1859), such tales have been best sellers around the world.

This fascination with forensic science is not difficult to understand. Investigators today have an amazing array of instruments, equipment, chemicals, and other devices with which to examine the most minute evidence. No criminal can hope to escape from a crime scene without leaving behind at least some evidence. A single eyelash may be all that is necessary for his or her *identification.*

One of the most important contributors to the forensic scientist's investigative arsenal has been the science of chemistry. Researchers have developed a host of new procedures for analyzing blood, fingerprints, DNA samples, documents, ammunition, medicines and drugs, soil, bacteria and other microorganisms, fire remnants, and even voiceprints. The purpose of *Forensic Chemistry* is to provide an introduction to some of the most important developments in this field over the past few decades and make it possible for readers to continue the study of forensic chemistry on their own.

Chapter 1 of the book provides a brief introduction to the history of forensic chemistry, describing some of the techniques that were used by investigators even before an authentic science of *criminalistics* existed. One of the most important breakthroughs of the period was the development of the Marsh test for arsenic, probably the first reliable and valid test for a toxic material available to forensic scientists. Chapter 2 deals with the long and fascinating history of fingerprinting. Dating to at least the third century B.C.E., fingerprinting was probably the first technique widely used by forensic scientists for the identification of wrongdoers. Over the past half century, a number of improvements in the way fingerprints are analyzed and identified have been made, many resulting from the use of chemical reactions.

The subject of chapter 3 is serology, the study of blood. The use of blood samples to identify individuals, for forensic or other purposes, dates to the discovery of blood types in 1901 by the Austrian physician Karl Landsteiner. Since that time, forensic scientists have expanded on Landsteiner's original discovery and developed a number of new techniques using chemical characteristics of blood molecules for identification purposes. Chapter 4 describes a field in which chemical research has had perhaps its greatest effect: the identification of drugs and poisons. The development of tests to identify specific drug elements and compounds has, of course, long been a major focus of chemical research. Research has produced test protocols that now make the recognition of illegal and dangerous substances a routine procedure in almost any crime investigation laboratory.

The power of chemical forensic chemistry is illustrated in chapter 5, which discusses arson and explosives investigations. Unraveling the history of an arson fire or explosion is a daunting task. By their very nature, such destructive events leave behind few traces. Yet forensic chemists have devised a number of ways of capturing, testing, and identifying minute amounts of fuels and other materials found at the scene of a fire or explosion. With these tools, investigators routinely apprehend perpetrators who likely imagined that they conducted their crime without leaving a trace of evidence behind.

Chapter 6 focuses on perhaps the newest and most exciting forensic procedure developed in modern history: *DNA typing*. With the development of techniques for enhancing microscopic pieces of DNA in the 1980s and 1990s, it has become possible to use samples as small as a single hair or a flake of skin to establish, with near certainty, the likelihood that a particular person has or has not committed a crime. The availability of DNA typing has already made possible the release of men and women convicted of crimes they did not commit and the apprehension of other men and women for crimes of which they were never suspected.

Television crime programs sometimes gloss over the challenges that have to be met in solving crimes; they usually have, after all, only an hour in which to tell their stories. Many crime investigations are far more complicated, requiring a variety of tests and long periods of analysis. Still, the crime programs do have it right in terms of the astonishing array of tools that investigators have at their disposal. Having read *Forensic Chemistry,* middle and high school students will possess an even better understanding of the chemical principles on which those tools are based and the way they are used in solving crimes.

1

THE ORIGINS OF
FORENSIC SCIENCE

"I've found it! I've found it," he shouted to my companion, running towards us with a test-tube in his hand. "I have found a re-agent which is precipitated by haemoglobin, and by nothing else."

These words were spoken by one of the most famous fictional detectives in the history of literature, Sherlock Holmes. In Sir Arthur Conan Doyle's first book about Holmes and his companion, Dr. Watson, *A Study in Scarlet* (1887), the great detective goes on to explain the significance of his discovery:

> "Why, man, it is the most practical medio-legal discovery for years. Don't you see that it gives us an infallible test for blood stains. . . . Beautiful! beautiful! The old Guiacum test was very clumsy and uncertain. So is the microscope examination for blood corpuscles. Now, this appears to act as well whether the blood is old or new. Had this test been invented, there are hundreds of men now walking the earth who would long ago have paid the penalty of their crimes."

Devising a test for blood was only one of Holmes's many skills in the field of forensic science. Later in the same book, he advises Scotland Yard in its search for a criminal who, he predicts, will be found to smoke a specific type of cigar, a Trichinopoly. When the suspect is later captured, Holmes explains that his deduction was simple because he had previously made a "modest study" of cigar ashes such that he could recognize more than a hundred specific examples of ash. The analytical skills given to Holmes by Conan Doyle were extensive and impressive. Indeed, in 2002, the Royal Society of Chemistry awarded Holmes an honorary fellowship, the first and only time a fictional character had been so recognized.

The Early Years of Forensic Science

Arthur Conan Doyle wrote at the beginning of a period that one historian has called "the century of the detective." That term refers to a time when criminologists first began to apply scientific principles to the solution of crimes. Sherlock Holmes's fictional forays into crime analysis coincided with a period during which real law enforcement officials were beginning to use fingerprints, blood samples, anthropometric characteristics, and other physical and biological traits to exonerate the innocent and convict the guilty in murders, assaults, burglaries, arsons, and other crimes.

The use of such evidence in crime analysis dates much earlier than the century of the detective. As far back as the eighth century C.E., for example, the practice of using fingerprints to identify and authenticate documents was introduced in China. Five centuries later, in 1248, a Chinese book entitled *Hsi Yüan Lu* (The washing away of wrongs) described a method by which a person's death by strangulation could be distinguished from death by drowning. *Hsi Yüan Lu* appears to be the first document in which a scientific principle is used to solve a crime.

With a few notable exceptions, the next seven centuries saw relatively little progress in the development of a scientific approach to crime analysis. One such exception resulted from the work of the famous Belgian chemist Jean Servais Stas (1813–91). Stas is best known in the history of chemistry for his work in determining the atomic weights of the elements. Less well known is his research on methods for detecting certain types of vegetable poisons in the body.

That work was inspired in 1851 by a notorious case in which Count Hippolyte de Bocarmé and his wife, Lydie, had become suspects in the murder of the countess's brother, Gustave Fougnies. The presiding magistrate in the case, a man by the name of Heughebaert, ordered that organs from Gustave's dead body be taken for examination by Stas, then a professor of chemistry at the University of Brussels and the leading chemist in the country. Upon examining those organs, Stas became convinced that the young man had been poisoned by a natural product, probably nicotine.

Nicotine had first been discovered and isolated from the tobacco plant *Nicotiana tabacum* in 1828. Its poisonous effects had been carefully studied, but no method had been found for detecting its presence in the human body. Meanwhile, its reputation as a highly poisonous material had become widespread, and it was thought to have been responsible for a number of unsolved murders.

In carrying out his analysis of Gustave's organs, Stas was able to devise a method for detecting the presence of nicotine in the body. He based his method on the fact that nicotine, like other *alkaloids,* is soluble in both alcohol and water. He first macerated the organs until they were reduced to a pulp, to which he then added a weak acid and alcohol. He then heated the mixture until the organic constituents of the organs were precipitated out, leaving behind in solution any alkaloids that might also be present. When he added water to the residue of this process, those alkaloids dissolved. Finally, he recovered the alkaloids (nicotine in this case) by allowing the water to evaporate. By examining the product of this series of reactions, Stas was able to identify the presence of nicotine in Gustave's organs, and Heughebaert was able to arrest and convict the Bocarmés of Gustave's murder.

The method developed by Stas was later modified and improved by the German chemist Friedrich Julius Otto (1809–70) at the University of Braunschweig. The test is still known as the Stas-Otto test and is used occasionally today for the identification of alkaloids in the body. It has, however, been replaced to a large extent by faster and more efficient spectrophotometric tests.

◄ SIR ARTHUR CONAN DOYLE (1859–1930) ►

The last quarter of the 19th century witnessed a rapid growth in a new field of science, the science of forensics. The work of researchers and law enforcement officials such as Jean Servais Stas, Ludwig Teichmann, Sir William Herschel, Izaak van Deen, Henry Faulds, Alphonse Bertillon, and Alexandre Lacassagne provided, for the first time in history, a solid scientific basis for the pursuit and conviction of criminals. It is somewhat surprising that, in the midst of this distinguished company of scholars, a leading name should be that of a fictional character, Sherlock Holmes, created by Arthur Conan Doyle.

Arthur Conan Doyle was born in Edinburgh, Scotland, on May 22, 1859, one of 10 children, seven of whom survived to adulthood. His father suffered from epilepsy and alcoholism and was eventually institutionalized, leaving his mother to manage the large family. Conan Doyle attended Jesuit schools in Lancashire, England, and Feldkirch, Austria, before enrolling in the medical program at the University of Edinburgh in 1876. Upon receiving his medical degree in 1881, he set up a medical practice in Plymouth with a fellow Edinburgh graduate, George Turnavine. After a short and turbulent partnership, Conan Doyle moved his practice to Southsea, where he had sufficient free time to begin writing fiction. His first story, *A Study in Scarlet,* appeared in *Beetons' Christmas Annual* for 1887, earning its author the princely sum of £25 (about $100 at the time). The success of *A Study in Scarlet* was sufficient to motivate Conan Doyle's continued interest in writing, and, in 1889, he published his first novel, *Micah Clarke.*

Over the next three decades, Conan Doyle vacillated between his commitment to additional short stories and novels about his most famous character, Sherlock Holmes, and his desire to produce more "substantial" works,

Advances in the 19th Century

By the mid-19th century, advances in forensic chemistry began to appear more rapidly. This period saw the development of tests for blood, the invention of the Marsh test for arsenic in 1832, and studies on bullet "fingerprinting" in the 1880s.

In 1863, the German-Swiss chemist Christian Friedrich Schönbein (1799–1868) discovered the first reliable method for identifying

primarily historical novels. The latter works benefited from and reflected his medical assignments overseas. In 1895, for example, he traveled to Egypt, where he hoped the climate would help cure his wife's bout of tuberculosis. The war that broke out that winter between the British and the Dervishes provided background for Conan Doyle's 1898 novel *The Tragedy of the Korosko*. Two years later, Conan Doyle was back in Africa again, this time serving as medical officer with the Middlesex Yeomanry in the Boer War. Again, this experience provided fodder for other books, especially the novels involving his second-most-famous character, Professor Challenger—*The Lost World* (1912) and *The Poison Belt* (1913).

Conan Doyle's fictional character Sherlock Holmes made forensic history by solving a series of apparently insoluble puzzles in more than two-dozen short stories and books, the first of which was *A Study in Scarlet*. Holmes continued to work his magic for seven years, until he was killed off by Conan Doyle in *The Final Problem,* published in 1893. At that point in his life, Conan Doyle had decided to put aside his interest in Holmes and turn his attention to more serious books that would, he hoped, make him a "lasting name in English literature."

Holmes's fans were devastated by Conan Doyle's decision, however. Many took to wearing black armbands when they read of Holmes's death, and more than 20,000 readers canceled their subscriptions to Holmes's literary home, the *Strand Magazine*. Upon further reflection, Conan Doyle decided to return to his most famous character in later short stories and books such as *The Hound of the Baskervilles* (1902), *The Return of Sherlock Holmes* (1905), *His Last Bow* (1917), and *The Case Book of Sherlock Holmes* (1927).

In recognition of his contributions to British literature, Conan Doyle was knighted in 1902. He died of heart disease at his home in Windlesham, Sussex, on July 7, 1930.

human blood. Schönbein found that hydrogen peroxide added to a bloodstain foams. This test was significant because blood deposited on clothing, wood, glass, or other surfaces soon dries to leave a brownish residue that is easily confused with other kinds of stains.

Another test for the presence of blood was developed at about the same time by a Dutch chemist by the name of Izaak van Deen. When van Deen put a West Indian herb called guaiac into contact with blood, the normally brownish herb changed color. The test continues to be used widely today for the detection of occult blood (blood that is not visible to the naked eye) in feces, although it is rarely used in forensic science.

For more than 12 centuries, arsenic has been popular as a poison. Its popularity dates from the eighth century, when the Arab alchemist Abu Musa Jabir Ibn Hayyan (ca. 721–ca. 815), also known as Geber, discovered a way of converting elemental arsenic (a gray, metallic-looking substance) into arsenious oxide (As_2O_3; a tasteless, odorless white powder). In the form of its oxide, arsenic could easily be added to a person's food or drink without causing suspicion. Moreover, until the 19th century, there was no way of detecting arsenic in the human body. As a result, the poison was widely popular among nearly all classes of people, from ordinary criminals to kings, queens, and popes. The notorious Borgia family is said to have been especially partial to the use of arsenic in eliminating its enemies.

As interest in forensic science grew in the 19th century, one of the first and most obvious problems posed for chemists was to find a way of detecting arsenic in the body, thus permitting prosecution of those who used it to commit murder. A number of forensic scientists and chemists, including Mathieu Joseph Bonaventure Orfila (1787–1853), the "father of toxicology," and Karl Wilhelm Scheele (1742–86), one of the discoverers of oxygen, searched for the solution to this problem. But the first to be successful was the British chemist James Marsh (1794–1846).

In 1832, when Marsh was employed as a chemist at the Royal British Arsenal in Woolwich, he was called to give expert testimony about the alleged poisoning of George Bodle. Marsh attempted to use a traditional test for arsenic in his testimony before the jury. In it, hydrogen sulfide gas is passed through a solution containing bodily fluids taken from the corpse. If arsenic is present in these fluids, the solution turns yellow.

The test showed a positive result, indicating that arsenic poisoning had occurred. Nonetheless, the jury found the defendant innocent. According to one observer, they were not convinced of Marsh's evidence because they had not actually *seen* the arsenic (a metallic, gray substance).

Marsh was infuriated not only by the jury's decision but also by the fact that the defendant later confessed that he had indeed poisoned Bodle. Marsh decided to develop a foolproof method for detecting arsenic that would convince even the most dubious observer. It took him four years to do so, but he was eventually successful. The test that he developed and that now carries his name is still used for the detection of arsenic samples with a mass of as little as 0.02 milligram.

The first step in the Marsh test is to add pure zinc metal and sulfuric acid to the sample to be tested. If arsenic (in the form of arsenious oxide) is present in the sample, it is reduced by the zinc:

$$As_2O_3 + 6Zn + 6H^+ \rightarrow 2As^{3-} + 6Zn^{2+} + 3H_2O$$

In this acidic solution, the resulting As^{3-} ions combine with hydrogen ions from the sulfuric acid to form a gas known as arsine (AsH_3):

$$As^{3-} + 3H^+ \rightarrow AsH_3$$

The arsine gas is then passed through a long, heated tube. Heat causes the arsine to decompose, yielding a silvery-black film of elemental arsenic and hydrogen gas:

$$2AsH_3 \xrightarrow{\text{(heat)}} 2As + 3H_2$$

The film of arsenic is sometimes called an *arsenic mirror*. Its size is directly proportional to the amount of arsenic contained in the original sample and can thus be used as a quantitative test for the amount of poison present in a body.

Marsh's test did not become an instantaneous, universal success. As other forensic scientists used it, a number of problems developed. For example, arsenic often occurs naturally with zinc. Thus, if impure zinc is used in the test, a positive (but misleading) result will be obtained. Over time, however, the testing procedure was refined and used with very pure materials. Eventually, it became one of the most highly respected of the early forensic tests developed by chemists. It is effective enough that it is used to the present day.

Nearly everyone today is familiar with the important role that fingerprints play in the identification of criminals (as well as in a host of other applications). Perhaps less well known is the parallel effort that forensic scientists have used for more than a century—to use the "fingerprints" of bullets to identify weapons used in crimes and the individuals who have used those weapons.

Possibly the earliest example of this research occurred in 1835 when an English police officer named Henry Goddard attempted to use the markings found on a bullet in a dead man's body to locate the man's murderer. Goddard was one of the last of the Bow Street Runners, the forerunners of today's Scotland Yard. He noticed that the bullet contained an unusual marking. He set out to find a mold from which a bullet with that kind of distinctive mark could have been made. When he was successful in locating that mold, its owner was so taken aback by the apparently irrefutable evidence that he confessed to the crime on the spot.

The Goddard story is of interest largely for historical reasons. Attempts to use bullet "fingerprinting" in criminal investigations were few and far between over the next 60 years. But by the 1890s, a combination of circumstances renewed interest in the technique as a way of identifying possible criminals.

Probably the most important of these factors was the introduction of a new method for making gun barrels, known as *rifling*. Rifling is the process by which spiral *grooves* are etched into the inner sur-face of a gun barrel. The grooves cause a bullet passing through the barrel to spin, and this rotational motion prevents the bullet from tumbling end over end once it leaves the gun barrel.

Various gun makers have used different systems of rifling. Some areas of difference are the number of grooves used in a barrel, the direction in which they spiral, the distance between adjacent spirals (called the *land*), and the angle of the spirals. The result is that each gun has a type of rifling that leaves a unique and characteristic set of marks on any bullet fired through it.

The first person to make an extensive study of the use of rifling patterns in criminal investigations was Alexandre Lacassagne (1843–1924), then professor of forensic medicine at the University of Lyon school of medicine. In 1889, he was called to investigate a murder in which a bullet had been removed from the victim's body. Lacassagne compared the markings on the bullet with the rifling pattern from a weapon owned by the chief suspect in the investigation. He concluded that the bullet was probably fired from the suspect's gun, providing a jury with sufficient evidence to convict the suspect.

As promising as this story may sound for the history of forensic science, it was only a beginning. Lacassagne studied only two characteristics of the rifling pattern—the number of grooves and the size of the lands. These characteristics are not sufficient to connect a specific gun with a bullet taken from a scene of a crime. So many different kinds of guns are made that additional markings are needed to obtain a positive connection between weapon and bullet.

Over time, methods for the "fingerprinting" of bullets became more sophisticated. In the 1920s, for example, a major in the U.S. Army named Calvin Goddard (1891–1955) invented an instrument called a comparison microscope with which the markings on two bullets could be compared with high specificity. A comparison microscope is simply a pair of optical microscopes mounted side by side on a common stand. The magnified images from the two microscopes are projected on adjacent screens so that they can be easily compared.

Bullet (or ballistic) "fingerprinting" became an issue of considerable interest in late 2002 when a pair of snipers killed and injured 13 individuals in the Washington, D.C., area. These crimes convinced a number of gun control advocates that all new firearms sold in the United States should be tested to produce a characteristic ballistic fingerprint. Such fingerprints could then be used, proponents argued, to trace the guns used in crimes by comparing bullets found at the crime scene with ballistic fingerprints on file at a central library.

At the time, two states, New York and Maryland, already had such laws on the books. Opponents of ballistic fingerprinting pointed out the enormity of the task involved in putting such a program in place, however. There may already be as many as 200 million firearms in the hands of Americans, almost none of which have been "fingerprinted" so far. No matter how useful ballistic fingerprinting may be, opponents say, the likelihood of turning it into a useful crime-solving tool is low.

The Scope of Forensic Chemistry

The analysis of a crime scene involves the participation of experts in both the physical and biological sciences as well as in many areas of technology and law enforcement. Forensic chemists study fingerprint patterns and fiber, glass, gunshot, and other types of residues; analyze drugs and poisons; examine possible forgeries; analyze residues for possible arson and explosive crimes; and carry out DNA analyses to identify possible criminal suspects.

Today the term *criminalistics* is often used to describe the work that forensic chemists and other forensic scientists do. The term means virtually the same as does the more common phrase *forensic science.* It has been defined by the California Association of Criminalists as follows:

> Criminalistics is that professional occupation concerned with the scientific analysis and examination of physical evidence, its interpretation, and its presentation in court. It involves the application of principles, techniques and methods of the physical sciences, and has as its primary objective a determination of physical facts which may be significant in legal cases.

In succeeding chapters of this book, a number of examples will be presented that illustrate the ways in which forensic chemists can contribute to the solution of crimes, with special emphasis on recent developments in techniques they use and the methods by which they work.

2

FINGERPRINTING

"When bloody finger-marks or impressions on clay, glass, etc., exist, they may lead to the scientific identification of criminals. . . . Already I have had experience in two such cases, and found useful evidence from these marks." This description of the potential use of fingerprints in crime detection was written by a Scottish doctor named Henry Faulds in a letter to the British science magazine *Nature* on October 28, 1880. At the time, Faulds was working as a missionary in Japan, where he had inadvertently been introduced to the traditional use of fingerprints by Japanese artisans to identify their work. Faulds became interested in the practice and was actually able to use it to discover that one of his medical students was responsible for the mysterious disappearance of alcohol from his laboratory. At first concerned about the reliability of fingerprinting as a detection device, Faulds eventually decided to seek the help of Charles Darwin in alerting the scientific world to the potential of dactylography, the use of fingerprints for the detection of crimes.

Faulds's letter is generally recognized as the first written statement about the role that fingerprints might have in the solution of crimes. The letter is by no means, however, the first occasion on which fingerprinting was suggested as a means of identifying individuals.

The History of Fingerprinting

The use of fingerprints to identify individuals can be traced at least as far back as the third century B.C.E., when the Chinese used such marks in legal disputes over business dealings and to claim ownership of a document or object. Historians do not know, however, whether the Chinese understood the distinctive nature of fingerprints.

Scientific studies of fingerprints began in the late 17th century when an English physician, Nehemiah Grew (1641–1712) took note of the "innumerable little ridges" that he observed on the tips of fingers. In an article he wrote for *Philosophical Transactions* in 1684, Grew noted: "If anyone will but take the pains, with an indifferent glass to survey the palm of his hand, he may perceive . . . innumerable little ridges, of equal bigness and distance, and everywhere running parallel one with another. . . . They are very regularly disposed into spherical triangles and elliptics." Grew made no effort in his paper, however, to suggest that the "innumerable little ridges" might serve any purpose in terms of identifying individuals.

The first concrete step in that direction occurred in 1823, when the Czech physiologist Jan Purkinjě (1787–1869) noted that fingerprints commonly followed one of nine distinctive patterns, which he called transverse curve, central longitudinal stria, oblique stripe, oblique loop, almond whorl, spiral whorl, ellipse, circle, and double whorl. Again, Purkinjě made no connection between these patterns and their potential use in the identification of criminals.

By the 1850s, however, the stage had been set for scientists and law enforcement officers to begin to see how fingerprints could be used in forensic science. One of the pioneers in this effort was William Herschel (1833–1918), the grandson of one of England's greatest astronomers. Herschel had been employed as assistant joint magistrate and collector for the British government in the Hooghly district of India. During his term of service in India, Herschel had found that retirees under his administration sometimes attempted to collect their pension payments more than once. To avoid being cheated by this practice, Herschel introduced a system of having each pensioner leave his thumbprint on a receipt to indicate that he had received payment.

Herschel remained involved in the study of fingerprints for the rest of his life. He was especially interested in discovering whether a person's prints changed over time, which, he decided, they did not. But he apparently had little interest at first in the possible use of fingerprinting as a forensic device. That changed, however, when he read Henry Faulds's letter to *Nature* in 1880. He responded with his own letter to the journal a month later, pointing out his own experience in fingerprint studies and suggesting that they might be used in dealing with criminal cases: "The ease with which the signature is taken and the hopelessness of either personation or repudiation are so great that I sincerely believe that the adoption of the practice in places and professions where such kinds of fraud are rife is a substantial benefit to morality."

As innocent as Herschel's letter may appear, it outraged Faulds, who thought that Herschel was trying to steal his priority for the discovery of fingerprinting as a forensic tool. Upon his return to England from Japan, Faulds attempted to interest police officials, not only in London, but also in New York, Paris, and other major cities of the world. He received, at best, polite dismissal. For all practical purposes, Faulds's research slipped quietly into the backwater of forensic science.

Within a decade, however, two important events established the role of fingerprinting in the arsenal of forensic science. The first was the 1892 publication of the first scientific book on fingerprinting, *Finger Prints,* by Sir Francis Galton (1822–1911), Charles Darwin's cousin. Galton drew heavily on the research of both Herschel and Faulds to develop a system by which the precise pattern of a set of prints could be used to identify its owner. Within a decade, law enforcement officers and criminal prosecutors were using Galton's book to find and convict criminals.

The second event was the development of the first workable system of fingerprint classification by the English police officer Sir Edward Henry (1850–1931) in 1900. Henry had read Galton's book and spoken with him in person about the potential of dactylography. When Henry was posted to India in 1896, where he served as inspector general of police for Bengal province, he assigned two officers to implement the Galton scheme in the region.

◄ SIR EDWARD HENRY (1850–1931) ►

The last quarter of the 19th century saw a surge in efforts to find ways of identifying individuals involved in criminal activity. Prior to that time, law enforcement officials were lucky to be able to say with any certainty which person among many possible suspects was guilty of a crime. There is little doubt that the great majority of wrongdoers escaped punishment because courts could not be convinced that they were, "without the shadow of a doubt," the guilty party. Probably the greatest step forward during this period was the development of finger-printing as a forensic tool. A pioneer in the emergence of this technology was Sir Edward Henry.

Edward Henry was born on July 26, 1850, at Shadwell, Wapping, London. He attended St. Edmund's College in Hertfordshire before en-rolling at University College, London, where he studied English, Latin, physics, and mathematics. After graduating in 1869, Henry took a po-sition as a clerk with Lloyd's of London, the famous insurance brokers. Two years later, he left that post to begin a study of law at the Society of the Middle Temple. In 1873, he accepted an appointment as assistant magistrate collector in the Bengal province of India.

Henry's interest in fingerprinting classification soon earned him notice at home, and in 1900, he was called to testify before the Belper Committee, a group organized to study problems of identifying crimi-nals for the London police. The committee was sufficiently impressed with Henry's work to send him to South Africa, where he organized the first fingerprinting bureau (consisting of one man) in the colony of Natal. A year later, he was recalled to England, where he was made assistant commissioner of Scotland Yard in charge of the Criminal Investigation Department. Within a month of assuming his new position, Henry had created the first fingerprint bureau at Scotland Yard.

In 1903, Henry was promoted to the post of commissioner of Scotland Yard, a position he held until 1918, when he resigned after a two-day strike by 11,000 police officers. He was knighted in 1906 and made a baronet in 1918. Henry died on February 19, 1931, at his home in Ascot, Berkshire.

Between July 1896 and February 1897, Henry and his two Bengali officers, Azial Haque and Hemchandra Bose, developed a system of fingerprint classification based on the pattern of *loops,* arches, and whorls found in fingerprints. The system made it possible to file, search, and compare fingerprints of thousands of individuals. By the end of 1897, Henry's system had been adopted by law enforcement agencies throughout British India. In 1900, Henry published a book describing his system, *Classification and Uses of Fingerprints,* that rapidly became a standard source for law enforcement agencies around the world. In 1901, he was recalled to England and appointed the first commissioner of Scotland Yard's new Fingerprint Bureau. The Henry system of fingerprint classification is still used largely in its original form in all English-speaking countries.

In less than a decade, the Henry system was adopted by most major police departments around the world. It became standard procedure for identifying criminals in the New York State prison system in 1903 and in the Leavenworth Federal Penitentiary and the St. Louis (Missouri) police department a year later. In 1905, the U.S. Army initiated fingerprinting as a standard procedure for all new recruits, and two years later, the U.S. Navy also adopted the policy. When the Federal Bureau of Investigation (FBI) was created by act of Congress in 1924, the new agency immediately began the process of collecting and filing fingerprint records currently available throughout the nation. The FBI is currently said to have more than 238 million fingerprints in its files (many of people long dead), about half of whom have been suspected or convicted of criminal activity.

General Principles of Fingerprinting

Fingerprints are characteristic features of human skin found on the palm side of the fingers and thumbs and on the soles of the feet. They are almost the only place on the body where the skin is not smooth. Biologists believe that fingerprints may have evolved to provide the hands and feet with rough surfaces that allow one to grasp and hold objects more easily.

Fingerprints begin to develop and are completely formed during the fetal stage of life. They have two fundamental characteristics that permit them to be used to identify an individual. First, fingerprint patterns are unique. No two humans have ever been found who have identical fingerprint patterns. Second, fingerprint patterns do not change during a person's lifetime. Attempts to sand down one's fingers, pour acid on them, or mutilate them in some other way in order to destroy or change the fingerprint pattern are doomed to failure; the pattern reappears once the skin grows back.

The basic structure of a fingerprint can easily be seen by means of a microscopic examination of skin patterns on the fingers, thumbs, and soles of the feet. The skin in such locations is folded into hills and valleys known respectively as *ridges* and *grooves.* The ridges are frequently referred to as *friction ridges,* because they provide the friction needed to grip and hold an object. Friction ridges may be of different lengths and shapes.

Scientists have now identified more than 150 different ridge characteristics (also known as *minutiae*) by which two fingerprint patterns can be compared with each other. For example, the ridges in a fingerprint pattern may be long in some places and short in another. They may be broken into short segments known as *islands.* They

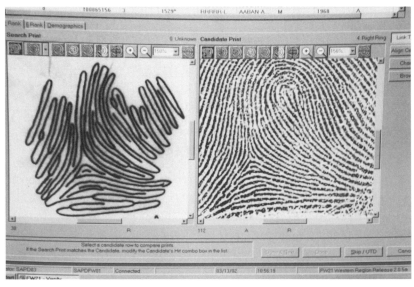

The most obvious features of a fingerprint are raised areas (ridges) and depressions (grooves). (Spencer Grant/Photo Researchers, Inc.)

may branch at some point in their length, producing *bifurcations.* And they may fold around upon themselves, forming closed loops.

One problem with the process of fingerprint identification is deciding how many of those 150 characteristics must match in order for the prints to be said to be identical. Law enforcement experts in the United Kingdom, for example, normally require two prints to match on 16 points in order for them to be considered identical. But that number is only 12 in Australia and New Zealand and 8 in India. Canada has no nationwide standard, and in the United States, each state sets its own standard, although the Federal Bureau of Investigation (FBI) uses a 12-point system. All of these systems are somewhat arbitrary since there is no scientific basis for deciding exactly how many matches are needed to provide a high level of confidence that a duplicate has been found.

The first legal challenge to the use of fingerprinting for the identification of possible criminals occurred in the case of *United States v. Byron Mitchell,* heard by the U.S. District Court for Eastern Pennsylvania in 1999. The defendant in that case argued that there was insufficient scientific evidence to permit identification based on fingerprint patterns. The court ruled for the prosecution in this case, providing at least a temporary legal basis for continued use of fingerprinting by law enforcement officers.

Fingerprints may take one of three forms: visible, plastic, or latent. Visible prints are left behind when a person transfers some type of colored material on his or her hand to a smooth surface by touching it. For example, a person's hands might become bloody during commission of a crime. That blood would then be left behind on any surface the individual touched, such as a door handle, tabletop, or automobile steering wheel. Paint, grease, dirt, ink, or other materials are also commonly found in visible prints.

Plastic prints are produced when a person touches a soft material, such as clay, mud, soap, or wax, in which the friction ridges produce a visible pattern. Latent prints are so called because they are invisible to the human eye. They are composed of eccrine secretions, produced by small sweat glands located just under the surface of friction ridges. Eccrine secretions are left behind after a person has touched an object. The vast majority of fingerprints that law enforcement officers deal with are latent prints. A number of chemical techniques have been developed by which such prints can be made visible and, therefore, usable for purposes of identification.

Fingerprinting Systems

The earliest attempt to devise a system for classifying fingerprints dates to Galton's 1892 book *Finger Prints*. In it, Galton suggested a scheme of categorization based on three main pattern types: arches, loops, and whorls. Each of a person's 10 fingers was assigned a letter indicating the most prominent pattern to be found there, an *A, L,* or *W*. The person's fingerprint "identity," then, consisted of a sequence of 10 letters, such as AALWL LLWLA, that could be filed alphabetically for future reference. Galton developed this system, not because he was interested in its possible application to the detection of crime, but because of his studies in racial characteristics and heredity. The scientific research for which he is best known today is in the field of eugenics, a science that attempts to improve the overall quality of the human race by selective breeding.

The first systems for the classification of fingerprints for law enforcement purposes were developed almost simultaneously by Sir Edward Henry in the United Kingdom and an Argentine police official, Juan Vucetich (1858–1925). Both systems were based largely on Galton's original research. Although the two systems are similar, they found separate audiences: Henry's eventually became popular primarily in the English-speaking world, and Vucetich's came to dominate in the Spanish-speaking world.

Since the Henry system still forms the basis on which most fingerprint classification systems are based today, it is explained here. In that system, the primary pattern observed on each finger is assigned a letter: *A* for arch, *W* for whorl, and *L* for loop, for example. Then, the 10 fingers are paired off as shown below:

1. Right index (RI) with right thumb (RT)

2. Right ring (RR) with right middle (RM)

3. Left thumb (LT) with right little (RL)

4.   Left middle (LM) with left index (LI)

5.   Left little (LL) with left ring (LR)

The presence or absence of a whorl (*only*) is noted for each finger. If a whorl appears on either or both of the first set of fingers, it is assigned a point value of 16. If it appears anywhere in the second set, it is given a value of 8. The presence of a whorl on any one of the last three sets is given a value of 4 (for the third pair), 2 (for the fourth pair), and 1 (for the fifth pair).

The total point value for the set of fingerprints is then determined by substituting the whorl point value for each finger in the following equation:

$$\text{Point value} = \frac{RI + RR + LT + LM + LL + 1}{RT + RM + RL + LI + LR + 1}$$

For a person with whorls on the right ring (RR), left middle (LM), and right little (RL) fingers, then, the point value assigned to his or her fingerprints would be:

$$\text{Point value} = \frac{0 + 8 + 0 + 2 + 0 + 1}{0 + 0 + 4 + 0 + 0 + 1} = \frac{11}{5}$$

The total number of different point values that can be calculated in this way is 1,024 (2^{10}). An investigator attempting to match fingerprints has his or her job reduced by 1/1,024 and, in this example, has to examine only those prints on file with a point value of 11/5.

Clearly, the above system does not provide a positive match between any two sets of fingerprints when there are tens or hundreds of millions of individuals living in a country. In the final analysis, some individual still has to sit down with two sets of prints, look at them very carefully, and discover how closely the minutiae of those prints actually match. If 16 points of match are found (in Great Britain), or 12 points (with the FBI), or some other number of points (with other agencies), then a match can be declared. The primary classification system described above, however, greatly simplifies that final stage of visual inspection.

The major challenge in the use of visual analysis of fingerprints is the time required to look for matching minutiae in two or more sets of prints. As early as the 1960s, the FBI began to explore the process of automating this process. The final result of that effort was the Integrated Automated Fingerprint Identification System (IAFIS), in which computer programs scanned and compared two or more sets of fingerprints at high speed. Today some variation of this system is used in nearly all law enforcement agencies in the United States and in many other parts of the world. Print matches are generally achieved in a matter of minutes or hours rather than a few weeks or a few months, the response time for comparable searches conducted by humans.

Fingerprint Detection

The use of fingerprint patterns to arrest and convict criminals has become a highly sophisticated, often complex procedure that makes use of the best tools available in the physical and chemical sciences. The specific procedure used depends on a number of crime scene variables and often involves a series of steps.

One of the most important variables affecting fingerprint identification (other than the prints themselves) is the kind of surface on which the prints are deposited. The procedure chosen for detecting and studying a print depends on whether the surface on which it was deposited is rough or smooth, porous or nonporous. In porous surfaces, the materials that make up the fingerprint (water and solids found in eccrine secretions) may soak into the material and migrate away from the area where they were left. A nonporous surface does not present this problem. The detection method used to analyze the print differs, therefore, for the two situations.

Investigators must also determine whether the surface holding the prints had previously been wet or not. Some components that make up a print are water soluble and would be dissolved on a wet surface, while others are not water soluble and would remain in place. Any colors or background patterns on a surface may also affect detection methods. Most chemical tests conducted on fingerprints result in the formation of a characteristic color for a positive test. With certain backgrounds, such as paper money, that color may be masked, necessitating a different test. The age of a fingerprint is also important. Some methods for identifying fingerprints detect only recently deposited prints, while others can detect prints that were made weeks or months earlier.

Fingerprint detection usually involves three major steps: locating the print, developing and/or enhancing its properties for better viewing, and protecting and preserving the print.

The basic principle behind fingerprint detection is the following: When a person touches a surface with his or her finger(s), a small amount of eccrine secretions from sweat glands on the hand is left behind on the surface, the fingerprint. That residue typically consists almost entirely (98.5 percent) of water, in which are dissolved small amounts (1.5 percent) of a large variety of solids. About two-thirds

◄ CHEMICALS COMMONLY FOUND IN ECCRINE SECRETIONS ►

ORGANIC	INORGANIC
Amino acids	Water (more than 98%)
Urea	Chlorides
Uric acid	Metal ions
Lactic acid	Sulfates
Monosaccharides and disaccharides	Phosphates
Creatinine	Ammonia
Choline	

of the solids are organic substances, while the remaining one-third is inorganic. The chart on page 21 lists some of the chemicals typically found in eccrine secretions. Although many of these substances are present in very small amounts, they are important because they may serve as the basis for some characteristic chemical reaction by which they, and therefore the fingerprint itself, may be detected.

Powder Tests

A latent fingerprint can be detected in any of three ways: with powders, by means of chemical tests, and by using optical procedures. It is not unusual for more than one test to be performed on a set of fingerprints, each more sensitive than the preceding, or each carried out for some specialized purpose. The following sections describe some of the most popular tests in use today. These tests are designed primarily for the detection of latent prints since visible and plastic prints typically do not require further enhancement to make them visible.

In the first procedure that is often used in the search for latent prints, the person collecting the print spreads a colored powder on it such that some of the powder adheres to the print, making it visible. The visible print can then be photographed or studied by other methods. The use of a powder is possible only when a relatively large amount of eccrine secretions has been deposited on a surface, at least 500 ng (ng = nanogram, 1 billionth of a gram).

Fingerprint powders come in many different colors, including black, white, gray, and red. Although black and gray tend to be the most common colors used, an investigator will select the color that provides the best contrast between the print and the surface it is on.

The process of testing for fingerprints with powders is relatively easy to learn but involves certain special skills. For example, the powder should be distributed carefully on the surface being studied to avoid damaging the print itself. The normal procedure is to sprinkle the powder on a camel's hair, nylon, or other fine-haired brush and then to wipe the brush gently across the surface being tested. Care is required because too much force on the surface may damage the fingerprint ridges, making the pattern more difficult to observe.

In some cases, the object or material on which the print has been deposited (for example, a pistol or knife) can be removed from the crime scene and taken to a crime laboratory for further study. In other cases, the print may be found on a surface that cannot be moved, such as a wall or a window. In that case, the investigator makes a copy of the print by gently placing a special kind of cellophane tape on the print. The powder on the print is transferred to the tape, which can itself be taken to a crime laboratory.

A variation of the powder detection method is called small particle reagent (SPR) analysis. This procedure can be used on wet surfaces, where the traditional dry powder method will not produce results. In an SPR analysis, the object on which the fingerprints have been deposited is submerged in an aqueous suspension of an insoluble solid in water. The particles of the solid stick to the organic portion of the prints (the eccrine secretions), producing an image, when dried, similar to that obtained from the dry powder approach.

One of the most sensitive powder-deposition methods currently available is vacuum metal deposition (VMD), illustrated in the diagram below. The method can be used when only very small amounts of print material have been left behind on a surface. The first step in the procedure is to place the surface being examined in a closed container

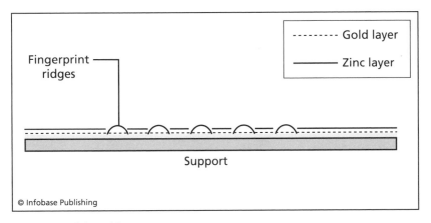

Vacuum metal deposition

from which air can be removed, creating a vacuum. A small sample of gold metal is then evaporated inside the container. Under these conditions, the gold adheres uniformly on the surface being studied. It forms a thin but consistent layer since it penetrates the fingerprint itself. Next, a small amount of zinc metal is evaporated within the container. The zinc adheres to the surface, on top of the gold, but does not adhere to any fingerprint material. The resulting "picture" consists of a uniform zinc background interrupted by "islands" of eccrine secretion-based materials that rejected the zinc coating.

Chemical Tests

The second method of fingerprint detection invokes some type of chemical test that results in the formation of a characteristic colored product. Chemical tests are more sensitive than powder tests and can generally be used with residues that weigh between 100 and 200 ng. Some of the most widely used chemical tests are the silver nitrate, iodine fuming, ninhydrin, superglue (cyanoacrylate), Physical Developer, and ruthenium oxide tests.

One of the oldest methods for the detection of latent fingerprints makes use of silver nitrate ($AgNO_3$). The test depends on the fact that silver nitrate reacts with the chloride ion present in eccrine secretions:

$$AgNO_3(aq) + Cl^-(aq) \rightarrow AgCl(s) + NO_3^-(aq)$$

When exposed to light, solid silver chloride readily decomposes, forming chlorine gas and solid, grayish silver metal:

$$2AgCl(s) + h\nu \rightarrow 2Ag^0(s) + Cl_2(g)$$

The test is familiar to most students of introductory chemistry classes and is one of the basic chemical reactions that takes place during the process of photography.

To perform the silver nitrate test, the tester sprays or gently wipes a small amount of a 3 percent solution of silver nitrate across the surface being examined for fingerprints. The surface is then exposed to ultraviolet light or, if that is not available, to bright normal light. Any fingerprints on the surface will become visible as a grayish pattern in a matter of minutes.

The silver nitrate test is used less frequently today than previously partly because the prints formed with the process tend to become blurred over time and are not usable with prints more than a few weeks old.

Another popular and widely used test for latent fingerprints is the iodine fuming test. When iodine crystals are heated, they sublime; that is, they pass directly from the solid to the vapor state without first melting. In the presence of eccrine secretions, the iodine reacts with fatty acids in the secretions, forming a brownish complex that is easily visible. The complex decomposes rather easily, however, and the brownish evidence of any prints present on a surface fades rather quickly.

The test is conducted by suspending the surface on which prints have been deposited in a closed container. Iodine crystals are heated in a separate container called an iodine fuming gun, and the vapors produced are passed into the closed container. The container must have a transparent front so that the results of the test can be easily seen and photographed. Any prints detected in this way can be "fixed," or made more permanent, by introducing a second reagent into the container. One substance commonly used is a starch solution, which reacts with iodine deposited on the prints to form a more permanent blue pattern.

Another fixing agent that is widely used is 7,8-benzoflavone (also known as naphthoflavone). When prints developed with iodine vapor are sprayed with a 0.3 percent solution of this chemical, the prints turn a dark purple that is retained longer than the original brownish tint from iodine alone. Iodine-benzoflavone spray kits are available for use in detecting latent prints directly at a crime scene. The kit contains a combination of iodine and benzoflavone that is mixed and then sprayed on walls, windows, or other surfaces where latent prints are suspected.

Ninhydrin is an aromatic compound whose systematic name is triketohydrindene hydrate. In 1910, the English chemist Siegfried Ruhemann (1859–1943) discovered that ninhydrin reacts with amino acids to form a distinctive purple compound now known as Ruhemann's purple. The test is conducted with a solution of about 0.5 percent ninhydrin in some appropriate solvent (such as ethanol or acetone). A number of different formulations are commercially available under names such as Arklone and Fluorisol. The solution is sprayed on the surface on which prints are suspected, and the appearance of the distinctive purple color is evidence of the existence of such prints. Color may begin to develop within a few hours or as long as 48 hours after application of the ninhydrin. Development of a ninhydrin print is also enhanced by heat treatment. The print-containing surface may be suspended in a heating oven at temperatures of up to 100°C for up to about five minutes.

The results of a ninhydrin test can be further enhanced and, in some cases, preserved by the addition of a second reagent. Spraying the print-containing surface with a salt of zinc, for example, causes a color change from purple to orange. In some cases, the color change permits the print pattern to stand out more clearly from the background than the original Ruhemann purple.

The ninhydrin test has now become the most popular test for latent fingerprints on paper. It has been used successfully in detecting prints that are up to 15 years old. Ninhydrin is by no means the only reagent that reacts specifically and characteristically with amino acids, however. A considerable amount of research has been conducted on analogs of ninhydrin, compounds with a chemical structure similar to that of ninhydrin and possessing a similar tendency to react with amino acids. Some of the compounds studied in this line of research produce results superior to those obtained with ninhydrin itself in fingerprint identification. These include benzo(f)ninhydrin; 1,8-diazafluoren-9-one (DFO); 5-methoxyninhydrin; and 5-(methylthio)ninhydrin.

In most cases, the ninhydrin analogues are superior, not because of the primary reaction between reagent (ninhydrin or ninhydrin analogue) and fingerprint, but because of the increased visibility of the print when viewed under optical light treatment. For example, DFO (1,8-diazafluoren-9-one) produces a pale pinkish-purple color when it comes into contact with amino acids. But, the prints can be made to fluoresce at room temperature in a relatively short period of time (less than 30 minutes). Another ninhydrin analogue with similar properties is 1,2-IND (1,2-indandione), which reacts with eccrine secretions to give a pale pink color. Under treatment with a strong light source, however, the print fluoresces with a strong green light. Yet another ninhydrin analogue, 5-MTN (5-[methylthio]ninhydrin), produces an even more pronounced purplish coloration than ninhydrin itself, and in addition, it fluoresces to give a pronounced orange color.

A popular commercial adhesive sold under the name of superglue has been shown to be an effective reagent for the detection of fingerprints. The primary ingredient of superglue is generally the methyl or ethyl ester of cyanoacrylic acid, methyl-2-cyanoacrylate or ethyl-2-cyanoacrylate. When superglue is heated, it produces a colorless vapor that appears to be especially attracted to oily products such as those generally found in a fingerprint. The vapor deposits on the ridge patterns of the fingerprint, polymerizes, and forms a white powder (polycyanoacrylate) that adheres to the prints.

The cyanoacrylate fuming test is easy to conduct. The object to be tested is suspended inside a container with at least one transparent side. A few drops of superglue or similar cyanoacrylate product is added to the container, and the container is sealed and heated to about 100°C. That heat is sufficient to cause vaporization and polymerization of the cyanoacrylate, resulting in the formation of distinctive white print patterns, a process that may take two hours or more. The cyanoacrylate fuming test has become the procedure of choice for the detection of latent prints deposited on nonporous objects, such as glass, plastic, rubber, and leather.

As with other methods of latent print detection, the prints obtained by means of the cyanoacrylate fuming test may be further enhanced by a variety of techniques for better viewing. They may be sprayed with a variety of dyes, such as gentian violet, basic yellow 40, basic red 28, rhodamine 6G, or thenoyl euoprium chelate. Sometimes the dye simply intensifies or otherwise improves the appearance of the print. Gentian violet, for example, combines with the white polycyanoacrylate powder deposited on a print to produce a deep purple. In other cases, the dye improves the fluorescence of the prints under an optical source. Prints treated with cyanoacrylate and then sprayed with Rhodamine 6G, for example, fluoresce strongly in the green region of the electromagnetic spectrum.

A product that has some important special applications in fingerprint identification is Physical Developer (PD). The primary active ingredient in PD is silver nitrate, a substance that reacts readily with chloride ions in eccrine secretions, as discussed earlier. The silver nitrate is mixed with an *oxidation-reduction* (redox) system, a detergent, and a buffer. A typical redox system consists of ammonium iron(II) sulfate [$Fe(NH_4)_2(SO_4)_2$] and iron(III) nitrate [$Fe(NO_3)_3$]. When PD is applied to a surface that contains fingerprints, silver ions adhere to the print ridges, where they are reduced to silver metal. As with the silver nitrate test already described, even very small amounts of silver metal are adequate to make prints visible.

The Physical Developer test has two special advantages. First, it works well with porous objects that are wet or that have been wet in the past. Second, PD has been effective in developing prints when other methods have been unsuccessful. The greatest disadvantage of the PD test, however, is that it is destructive. The chemicals in the product may wash away parts of the print itself or may react with the surface to which they have adhered. It must, therefore, be the final test carried out on a sample.

Latent fingerprints occur on such a wide variety of materials and under such a wide variety of circumstances that specialized tests can sometimes produce results that more traditional procedures (such as ninhydrin, cyanoacrylate, and silver nitrate tests) might miss. For example, dimethylaminocinnamaldehyde (DMAC) has been used for the detection of prints left on thermal paper, a material that has posed problems with other detection systems. DMAC reacts with urea in eccrine secretions to produce a dark red product.

Another test showing some promise has involved the use of ruthenium tetroxide (RuO_4). Since ruthenium tetroxide presents certain safety hazards (it tends to decompose explosively above 200°F [100°C]), historically its use has been quite limited. In 1995, however, a team of Japanese researchers developed a safe method by which the reagent can be used. It is now available in that formulation under the name of RTX. When a material is exposed to RTX fumes, any fingerprints on it will react with the reagent to produce a dark gray image. The reagent has proved to be especially useful on certain types of porous materials, such as paper money, that pose problems for other types of detection systems.

Light Tests

Fingerprints that are normally not visible under ordinary light may often be seen if the light or the object being viewed is modified in some way. One of the simplest modifications of light to reveal a latent print is simply to shine a strong line source at an oblique angle to the surface. In some cases, this change in the direction of light alone may reveal a print that was otherwise not visible. In other cases, using a different type of light source may reveal prints. An instrument known as the Reflected Ultraviolet Imaging System (RUVIS), for example, emits an ultraviolet light that is directed at a surface suspected of holding latent prints. Prints otherwise not visible in ordinary light may become visible under the ultraviolet beam.

In the 1970s, an important discovery revealed that exposure to laser beams may cause latent fingerprints to fluoresce. Fluorescence occurs when an atom absorbs a photon of energy, which is then used to raise one of its electrons to a higher level. After a brief moment, the electron returns to its ground level, emitting a second photon of energy with a wavelength and frequency different from that of the incident light.

Lasers are often useful in producing fluorescence of latent fingerprints because they provide an intense monochromatic beam of light (that is, light of a single wavelength). In order to be effective, the laser must be "tuned" to the frequency of the electron transition that takes place in atoms of the prints being sought. In 1977, Brian Dalrymple, a forensic analyst with the Ontario Provincial Police, and his colleagues discovered that light from an argon laser was ideal for this purpose. An argon laser produces light with a wavelength of about 480 nm, in the blue-green portion of the electromagnetic (EM) spectrum. Atoms in a latent print absorb the light and reemit it with a new wavelength of about 550 nm, in the yellow-green portion of the EM spectrum. By accident, Dalrymple and his team found that the protective safety goggles worn by laser operators filtered out

◄ BRIAN DALRYMPLE (1947–   ) ►

Nonspecialists are familiar with film and television depictions of finger-print detection, in which a detective brushes fingerprint powder across surfaces at a crime scene, sometimes with spectacular results. But fingerprint analysis has become a far more sophisticated procedure than this. Prints are often treated and analyzed by a series of tests, each more sensitive than the preceding. One of the great breakthroughs in fingerprint identification was the discovery that, when exposed to the proper optical conditions, fingerprints may fluoresce, providing a more vivid and detailed print pattern than may be available with traditional physical and chemical techniques. A pioneer in the study of optical methods of fingerprint analysis is Brian Dalrymple.

Brian Ellsworth Dalrymple was born in Toronto on September 23, 1947. He attended the Ontario College of Art, from which he received his bach-elor's degree in 1970. He then attended the Ontario Police College and the Sheridan College of Applied Arts & Technology, where he studied biologi-cal photography. He joined the Ontario Provincial Police in 1980, where he served as a forensic analyst. He was later promoted to senior forensic ana-lyst (1980–92) and, later, to manager of the Forensic Identification Services

extraneous wavelengths of radiation, allowing the light emitted by the fingerprint to be seen with special clarity.

A number of adaptations have been made to this procedure, but the basic principle remains the same. Different types of light can be used to produce fluorescence in a fingerprint, and the print may be treated in various ways to cause or enhance fluorescence. And a variety of filters for the safety goggles worn in the test can be used to make the reemitted light more vivid.

One of the most important of these developments was the dis-covery that traditional fingerprint tests (such as the ninhydrin or cyanoacrylate test) could be made more useful by adding a second chemical to a print being examined to make it fluorescent or to en-hance its fluorescence. Some common examples are the use of zinc or cadmium chloride following the ninhydrin test and the use of rhodamine 6G after the cyanoacrylate test.

(1992–98). From 1998 to 1999, he served as a special projects consultant to the office of the Ontario chief coroner's office. In 1999, he established his own consulting firm, Forensic Consulting.

While a member of the Ontario Provincial Police department in the 1980s, Dalrymple and his colleagues studied the inherent luminescence produced by fingerprints under certain conditions, the effect of using lasers and other various kinds of light sources for the illumination of prints, the use of specialized safety goggles for the viewing of luminescence, the computer enhancement of fingerprint patterns, and a number of other topics relating to the analysis and enhancement of prints.

Dalrymple has been an expert witness for cases heard in courts in Ontario, Quebec, Alberta, New York State, and Bermuda. He has taught forensic science at a number of law enforcement venues, including the Ontario Police College, the Michigan State Police, the Royal Canadian Mounted Police, the Israel Police Force, the University of Toronto, the University of New Haven, the International Association for Identification, the Sir Sandford Fleming College, and the Niagara Regional Police Service. Dalrymple has been awarded the John Dondero Award of the International Association for Identification, the Foster Award of the Canadian Identification Society, and the Lewis Minshall Award of the United Kingdom's Fingerprint Society.

Another important discovery was the finding that lasers are not required to produce luminescence; in fact, ordinary light is often satisfactory for developing or enhancing fingerprints. The primary requirement is that the light must be sufficiently intense to cause a print to fluoresce visibly. A variety of such light sources has been tried, and many have become part of the forensic scientist's crime-detection arsenal. High-intensity light sources used for the fluorescence of latent prints are commonly known as forensic light sources.

The search for new methods of detecting, enhancing, and preserving fingerprints continues in forensic science. There are always opportunities for discovering methods of uncovering prints that cannot be easily found by existing methods or for improving the efficiency of methods that have been known and used for long periods of time.

3

FORENSIC SEROLOGY

"For by their blood shall ye know them."
—With apologies to Matthew 7:20

One of the cardinal doctrines of forensic science is that criminals always leave trace evidence—"clues"—behind at the scene of a crime. In the case of many violent crimes, such as murders and rape, the most valuable type of evidence is likely to be blood.

Blood is important because certain characteristics of blood are variable in the human population. When evidence of a crime includes blood samples, these variations can help identify who could or could not have committed it. Investigators can also gain important insights to a crime by studying the patterns of any associated bloodstains. Before accomplishing any of this, however, it may be necessary to find out whether a sample under investigation is actually human blood.

Scientists who study blood and other bodily fluids for evidence in the analysis of a crime are known as forensic serologists. Relatively little research was done in the field of forensic serology prior to the 20th century. As mentioned in chapter 1, two tests were developed in the 1860s for the detection of blood and its primary protein component, hemoglobin: the guaiac test (van Deen in 1862) and the hydrogen peroxide test (Schönbein in 1863). Mathieu Orfila, the "father of toxicology," also studied the possibility of analyzing blood and semen stains by using a microscope.

But the real origins of forensic serology can be traced to the work of the Austrian-American physician Karl Landsteiner (1868–1943). In 1901, Landsteiner announced that human blood can be classified into only a few general classes or types, which are known today as A, B, AB, and O.

Blood Types

Landsteiner began his research because he was interested in finding out why it is not possible to transfuse blood from any one human into any other human (or, for that matter, from a nonhuman animal into a human). Physicians had long believed that blood was blood. It should be possible, they thought, to remove the blood from one person and give it to any second person who had been injured or wounded and needed additional blood.

But physicians had also learned that this simple idea was not true. In some (but not all) cases, a person who received a blood transfusion from another person became very ill and died. Today we know what happens in such "failed" transfusions. The blood cells from the donor begin to agglutinate, or clump together. The agglutinated cells can then block blood vessels and stop the flow of blood throughout the body. The agglutinated cells may also crack open, releasing their contents into the recipient's bloodstream. Some of those contents are toxic and can cause the recipient to die. For example, hemoglobin, the core protein in red blood cells, is toxic to the body once it has been removed from a red blood cell.

The process by which agglutination occurs is now well understood. Blood is a complex mixture of cells, cell fragments (platelets), protein molecules, and inorganic ions suspended and dissolved in a pale yellowish liquid called plasma. For the purposes of blood typing (and other problems in forensic serology), the most important component of blood is red blood cells (RBCs), the cells that are responsible for transporting oxygen from the lungs to cells throughout the body. The color of red blood cells is due to the presence of the protein hemoglobin.

The surface of red blood cells is covered with many different kinds of molecules. These molecules serve a variety of purposes,

---

◄ MATHIEU JOSEPH BONAVENTURE ORFILA (1787–1853) ►

Historians are in almost unanimous agreement that the title of "father of toxicology" can be given to a single person, Mathieu J. B. Orfila. Orfila was born in Mahón, on the Spanish island of Minorca, on April 24, 1787. At the age of 15, he signed on as a seaman for a voyage that was to take him to Sardinia, Sicily, and Egypt. Instead of marking the beginning of a career at sea, the voyage convinced Orfila that he was not suited to life on ships. Instead, he decided to pursue a career in medicine, studying at both the University of Valencia and the University of Barcelona. He proved successful enough in his studies to earn a grant allowing him to continue his education at the University of Madrid and, later, at the University of Paris.

While Orfila was in Paris, the Peninsular War (1808–14) broke out in Spain, preventing him from returning to his homeland. Fortunately, he was able to obtain the assistance of the French chemist Louis Nicolas Vauquelin (1763–1829), which allowed him to remain in France and continue his studies. Orfila remained in Paris for the rest of his life. He completed his work for a medical degree and, in 1819, was appointed professor of medical jurisprudence at the University of Paris. Four years later, he was appointed professor of chemistry in the school of medicine at Paris, replacing his longtime friend and benefactor, Vauquelin.

---

such as transmitting messages to other cells and molecules in the surrounding environment and receiving messages from those cells and molecules. RBCs differ to some extent in different individuals. For example, the RBC surfaces of two people—designated Ms. V and Mr. W—might present the following patterns, where each number represents a different kind of molecule:

Ms. V: 323, 415, 278, 199, 301, 894, 111, 300, 793, 232, 109
Mr. W: 323, 489, 278, 199, 301, 894, 771, 300, 443, 232, 109

If blood is transferred from Ms. V into Mr. W., the latter's body will not recognize Ms. V's RBCs because they do not match his own RBC patterns. His body will treat them as "foreign invaders" that represent a threat to Mr. W's body. Mr. W's immune system will

During the 1830s and 1840s, Orfila earned a number of honors. He was made dean of the faculty at the University of Paris, a member of the council of education of the French government, and a commander of the Legion of Honor.

Orfila is credited with establishing many of the basic principles of modern toxicology. He is probably the first person to have conducted experiments on the effects of poisons, using dogs and other animals for his research. Orfila compiled the results of his research as well as his other thoughts on toxicology in the first textbook written on the subject, *Traité des poisons* (*Treatise on Poisons*, 1813). His other books dealt with medical chemistry: *Elements de chimie medicate* (*Elements of Medicinal Chemistry*, 1830); studies of exhumed bodies: *Traité des exhumations juridiques* (*Treatise on Legal Exhumations*, 1830); and the toxic effects of arsenic: *Recherches sur l'empoisonnement par l'acide arsenieux* (*Research on Poisoning by Arsenians Acid*, 1841). Orfila was also called frequently as an expert witness in criminal trials involving the use of poisons.

With the installation of the republican government in 1848, however, Orfila fell out of favor, a circumstance that biographers say may have shortened his life. In any case, he died in Paris on March 12, 1853, after a short illness.

spring into action and begin releasing molecules that will attack and destroy the "foreign invaders": Ms. V's RBCs. These attacking molecules are antibodies. For each specific molecule unfamiliar to a person's immune system—molecules known as *antigens*—the immune system will produce a specific antibody.

The chemical nature of the antigens responsible for the blood types that make up the ABO blood groups was first discovered in 1953 by two English biochemists, Walter Morgan (1900–2003) and Winifred Watkins (1924–2003), then at the Lister Institute. All three antigens have remarkably similar structures that contain a single molecule of glucose (Glu in the diagram on page 36) attached to a molecule of galactose (Gal), a molecule of N-acetylglucosamine (Nag), another molecule of galactose, and a molecule of fructose (Fru):

—lipid tail—Glu—Gal—Nag—Gal—Fru

In that conformation, the structure acts as an O antigen. If a molecule of N-acetylgalactosamine is added to the terminal galactose molecule, the structure acts as an A antigen. If a molecule of galactose is added to the terminal galactose molecule, the structure acts as a B antigen. This description makes clear how the difference of only a few atoms distinguishes between the three antigen structures found on RBCs.

A antigen: —lipid tail—Glu—Gal—Nag—Gal—Fru
                                                                |
                                                              Nag

B antigen: —lipid tail—Glu—Gal—Nag—Gal—Fru
                                                                |
                                                              Gal

This background provides a basis for understanding the four blood types that Landsteiner first recognized more than 100 years ago. The chart on page 37 summarizes the essential properties of each blood type. Notice in this chart that a person who has type A blood is so classified because the surface of his or her RBCs has an "A" antigen. Such a person also has antibodies that do not recognize and, therefore, attack type B blood cells. They are anti-B antibodies.

A person with type A blood who receives type A blood from a donor, then, is at no risk because the recipient's body "recognizes" and accepts the type A blood. If the same person is given type B blood, however, his or her immune system does not "recognize" the type B blood cells, and its anti-B antibodies begin to attack the transfused blood.

Similar logic can be used to decide what kinds of blood an individual can donate or accept, based on the blood types of the donor and recipient. That information is summarized in the chart on page 38.

The physical process of testing for ABO blood types is actually quite simple and requires only two reagents, anti-A *serum* and anti-B serum. The blood sample to be identified is tested with each reagent, one at a time. The chart on page 39 shows what results may occur and what information each result provides. In the first case, if the

◀ PROPERTIES OF FOUR BLOOD TYPES ▶

BLOOD GROUP	ANTIGENS ON RBCs	ANTIBODIES IN SERUM*	FREQUENCY IN POPULATION
A	A	anti-B	40–42%
B	B	anti-A	10–12%
AB	AB	neither anti-A nor anti-B	3–5%
O	neither A nor B	both anti-A and anti-B	43–45%

*Serum is the clear, liquid part of the blood that remains after blood cells and clotting proteins have been removed.

sample tests positive (produces agglutination) with anti-A serum but negative (no agglutination) with anti-B serum, the blood is considered type A. A negative result with anti-A serum and a positive result with anti-B serum, by contrast, indicates that the blood is of type B. Finally, positive or negative tests with both reagents indicates the presence of type AB or type O, respectively.

So how does all this information about blood typing help to solve crimes? Suppose that a forensic scientist is able to collect a sample of blood from a crime scene and determine that it is type A blood. Immediately, that information narrows the number of possible suspects for the crime. Notice from the chart above that about 40 percent of humans have type A blood. So the number of all possible suspects is reduced (at least in theory) from 100 percent (everyone) to about 40 percent (those with type A blood). More important, if a person suspected of the crime has type B blood, then he or she can probably be deleted from the list of suspects.

◄ RULES FOR BLOOD TRANSFUSIONS ►		
BLOOD GROUP	CAN GIVE BLOOD TO	CAN RECEIVE BLOOD FROM
A	A and AB	A and O
B	B and AB	B and O
AB	AB	A, B, AB, and O
O	A, B, AB, and O	O

But narrowing the field of suspects from 100 percent to 40 percent probably does not help very much. Fortunately, more than one system of blood typing has been discovered. That is, individuals' RBCs differ from each other by more than a single molecule. A second system of blood typing with which many people are familiar is the Rh system, named for the blood factors (Rh+ and Rh-) that were first observed in rhesus monkeys.

The Rh factor is another distinguishing characteristic of an individual's blood. It is possible to combine two different and independent blood characteristics (the ABO type and the Rh type) to get a new set of probabilities. For example, the probability of a person being both type O and Rh+ is about 39 percent. The probability of an individual being both type AB and Rh+ is about 4 percent. The chart on page 40 shows a more common method for expressing the probability of finding a person with various combinations of these two different blood groupings. As the chart shows, the availability of two systems of blood typing increases the possibility of identifying a blood sample. Instead of matching only one blood type (such as the ABO system), a blood sample must match two blood types (such as ABO and Rh systems). Investigators can be more certain that a suspect of a victim matches on two blood criteria rather than one.

◁ TESTING FOR BLOOD TYPES ▷

RESULTS PRODUCED WHEN ANTI-A SERUM IS ADDED	ANTI-B SERUM IS ADDED	ANTIGEN PRESENT	BLOOD TYPE
+	-	A	A
-	+	B	B
+	+	A and B	AB
-	-	neither A nor B	O

Over the past half century, immunochemists (chemists who study substances found in the immune system) have discovered a number of other antigen-antibody systems in blood. The International Society of Blood Transfusion (ISBT) currently recognizes 26 such blood-grouping systems. In addition to the ABO and Rh systems, such groupings include the MNS, Lutheran, Kell, Lewis, Duffy, Kidd, Diego, Cartwright, Xg, and Scianna systems. All operate on the same general principle as the ABO system, and all give another test by which the probability of identifying a suspect can be improved. Suppose, for example, that a particular blood sample has been found to have an ABO type of B, an Rh type of +, and an MNS type of Ms (frequency of 0.31). Then the probability of a particular individual having all three of these blood types would be the product of their individual frequencies, or:

$$0.10 \text{ (B)} \times 0.86 \text{ (Rh+)} \times 0.31 \text{ (Ms)} = 0.027$$

This number means that for every 100 people, 2.7 will have the given combination of blood factors. In other words, the chance of

◁ **EXPECTED FREQUENCY OF INDIVIDUALS WITH TWO BLOOD TYPES (ABO AND RH GROUPS)** ▷

BLOOD TYPE	EXPECTED FREQUENCY
A+	1 in 3
A-	1 in 16
B+	1 in 12
B-	1 in 67
AB+	1 in 29
AB-	1 in 167
O+	1 in 3
O-	1 in 15

any one person having that combination is 100 ÷ 27, or 1 in 37. The use of a number of blood factors, rather than the one ABO system developed by Landsteiner, narrows down significantly the number of individuals who must be considered as a suspect or victim in a crime.

Polymorphic Proteins and Isoenzymes

Of the 26 ISBT blood-typing systems available today, only the ABO and Rh systems are commonly used in forensic serology. In order to specify more precisely the characteristics of a blood sample, a serologist is likely to analyze other components found in blood, primarily *polymorphic* proteins or isoenzymes. Polymorphic proteins

◁ SOME PROTEINS AND ENZYMES USED IN BLOODSTAIN ANALYSIS ▷

ABBREVIATION	PROTEIN OR ENZYME
ADA*	Adenosine deaminase
AK*	Adenylate kinase
EAP*	Erythrocyte acid phosphatase
EsD	Esterase-D
G-6-PD*	Glucose-6-phosphate dehydrogenase
GLOI	Glyoxylase I
GPT	Glutamic pyruvate transminase
Hp	Haptoglobin
PeP A	Peptidase A
PGM*	Phosphoglucomutase
6-PGD*	6-Phosphogluconate dehydro-genase
Tf	Transferrin

are proteins found in blood that occur in more than one form. Of course, enzymes are a kind of protein, so this distinction is some what irrelevant chemically, but it is widely acknowledged among forensic serologists.

◀ PHILIP LEVINE (1900–1987) ▶

When one mentions the term *blood typing*, a famous name springs to mind almost immediately: Karl Landsteiner. In the early 1900s, Landsteiner discovered that human blood could be classified into specific categories, or *types* (such as A, B, AB, and O), an accomplishment for which he received the 1930 Nobel Prize in physiology or medicine. Landsteiner spent much of the rest of his life looking for other ways of classifying blood. Over the next three decades, he was also involved in the discovery of the Rh, MNS, LW, and P blood systems. But Landsteiner did not work alone on these research projects. He shares credit for many of his discoveries with other immunologists, one of whom was Philip Levine.

Philip Levine was born in the small village of Kletsk, Russia, on August 10, 1900, the sixth of seven children. In fear of anti-Semitic attacks and pogroms, his family immigrated to the United States when Philip was eight years old. The family settled in Brooklyn, where Levine attended public schools. He then enrolled at the City College of New York, from which he received his bachelor of science degree in 1919. After serving briefly in the U.S. Army, just as World War I was coming to an end, he began medical training at Cornell University Medical College, which granted his M.D. degree in 1923. Two years later, he added an M.A. degree for advanced work in the field of immunology.

A major turning point in Levine's academic career came in 1925, when he was asked to join Landsteiner as assistant at his new research laboratory at the Rockefeller Institute. There he helped develop Landsteiner's ABO blood

---

Polymorphic proteins and isoenzymes are proteins that are chemically distinct from, but functionally similar to, each other. That is, their molecular structures differ in one or more ways, but they carry out essentially the same biochemical or biological function. Until the early 1960s, most biochemists believed that nearly all proteins were monomorphic; that is, they had only one structure. Then researchers began reporting a number of exceptions to that general rule. In 1963, for example, the English biologist David A. Hopkinson reported that the enzyme erythrocyte acid phosphatase (EAP) has

system and was codiscoverer of the MN and P blood systems. Landsteiner later credited Levine with influencing the way he carried out his research, adhering to the highest standards of careful work practices and logical thinking. Landsteiner is reported to have told Levine late in his life, "Dr. Levine, you do not know how to tell a lie," which Levine took as one of the highest compliments he had ever received.

In 1932, Levine accepted an appointment at the University of Wisconsin, where he turned his attention to a study of bacteriophages as part of an agreement with Landsteiner that he would discontinue his research on blood groups. Three years later, Levine had returned to the East Coast, where he took a position as bacteriologist and serologist at the Newark Beth Israel Hospital in New Jersey. In 1939, Levine observed a case in which a young mother delivered a stillborn child and then developed a severe reaction when transfused with blood from her husband. The case caused Levine to begin thinking about possible blood factors that might lead to such a result. And that, in turn, led to Landsteiner's and Alexander Wiener's 1940 discovery of Rh factors in blood, which eventually led to tests that now save the lives of countless women whose Rh factors do not match those of their fetuses.

In 1944, Levine moved to the newly established Ortho Research Foundation in Raritan, New Jersey, where he founded a center for blood group research. He retired from Ortho in 1965, at which time his research laboratory was renamed the Philip Levine Laboratories. Levine continued to work at Ortho in an emeritus position until 1985 and as a consultant, researcher, and author until his death on October 18, 1987, in Manhattan.

three isomeric forms. He called these P(a), which has a frequency in the general population of about 35 percent; P(b), with a frequency of about 60 percent; and P(c), with a frequency of about 5 percent.

Since then, a number of other polymorphic proteins and isoenzymes have also been discovered. Today biochemists have come to expect some polymorphism in such molecules and believe that as many as 40 percent of all genes are capable of producing polymorphic protein products. Forensic serologists have taken advantage of this advance and developed tests for a number of polymorphic proteins and isoenzymes. Some of the most common of those substances are listed in the chart on page 41. The six systems marked with an asterisk are the ones used most widely by forensic serologists today.

Of the 12 substances listed in the chart, 10 are isoenzymes. (The name of an enzyme can be recognized by the characteristic suffix -*ase.*) The other two substances are polymorphic proteins. Haptoglobin is a protein that binds to hemoglobin when it is released from a red blood cell, thereby preventing the loss of hemoglobin from the body. The transferrins are glycoproteins (compounds that contain both sugar and protein components), which transfer iron in the blood.

The frequency distribution for each of the polymorphic forms of each of the proteins and enzymes listed in the chart is known. So the probability that a blood sample comes from some given individual can be calculated in essentially the same way as for blood typing in the last section. The chart below shows how this might be done for an imaginary case in which blood typing was done for a number of factors.

◁ SAMPLE CALCULATION OF FREQUENCIES BASED ON TYPICAL BLOOD SPECIMEN ▷

BLOOD GROUP SYSTEM	TYPE	FREQUENCY	CUMULATIVE FREQUENCY
ABO	B	12%	12%
Rh	-	15%	12% × 15% = 1.8%
ADA	1	90%	1.8% × 90% = 1.6%
6PGD	A	96%	1.6% × 96% = 1.6%
Tf	DD	1%	1.6% × 1% = 0.016%

Notice that the total cumulative frequency is the combination of all blood factors occurring in an individual; it is equal to the product (p) of the individual frequencies:

$$p = 0.12 \times 0.15 \times 0.90 \times 0.96 \times 0.01 = 0.00016$$

In this example, the combination of blood factors is rare, to be expected in only about one out of 6,250 individuals ($1 \div 0.00016$) in the general population. This result is somewhat atypical, partly because the blood contains at least one very rare polymorphic form, the DD form of the transferrin (Tf) system.

Most of the blood tests described thus far have been developed for use in criminal cases, often cases involving a violent crime. But such tests can also be used in settings that involve civil rather than criminal cases. Perhaps the most common example involves the issue of paternity, determining the identity of the father of a child.

Although there is never a problem in identifying the mother of a child, it is not unusual for there to be a question as to the child's father. Blood tests can provide a partial answer as to the paternity of a child, but one that has a high degree of uncertainty.

Based on the laws of genetics, for example, it is possible to say that a child with type AB blood born to a woman with type A blood cannot be the child of a man with type A blood. (Neither mother nor father could then have supplied the B component of the child's blood.) On the other hand, a child with either type A blood or type O blood could be the offspring of a man with type A blood. In this case, blood testing cannot be used to decide who the father is, although it can prove who is not the father. The genetic combinations that are possible are shown in the chart on page 46.

A useful adjunct to classic ABO blood testing in determining paternity is the human leukocyte antigen (HLA) test. This test is based on a discovery made in 1958 by the French medical researcher Jean Dausset (1916–   ). Dausset elucidated the essential elements involved in the operation of the human immune system, including the discovery of a class of compounds known as human leukocyte antigens. These antigens (molecules one's immune system does not recognize) exist on white blood cells, in contrast to almost all other polymorphic proteins and isoenzymes used by forensic serologists

◄ PATTERNS OF GENETIC TRANSMISSION IN BLOOD TYPES ►

MALE TYPE	O				A				B				AB			
FEMALE TYPE	O	A	B	AB	O	A	B	AB	O	A	B	AB	O	A	B	AB
CHILD TYPE																
O	Y	Y	Y	N	Y	Y	Y	N	Y	Y	Y	N	N	N	N	N
A	N	Y	N	Y	Y	Y	Y	Y	N	Y	N	Y	Y	Y	Y	Y
B	N	N	Y	Y	N	N	Y	Y	Y	Y	Y	Y	Y	Y	Y	Y
AB	N	N	N	N	N	N	Y	Y	N	Y	N	Y	N	Y	Y	Y

Y = Man *may* be parent of child
N = Man *cannot* be parent of child

in testing blood samples. HLAs were later found to be polymorphic, providing serologists with one more system for distinguishing blood types from each other.

Four major classes of human leukocyte antigens exist: HLA-A, HLA-B, HLA-C, and HLA-D. Each of these, however, includes a number of subclasses, polymorphic forms of the human leukocyte antigen. There are 23 known types of HLA-A, 47 types of HLA-B, eight types of HLA-C, and 14 types of HLA-D. In paternity testing, then, the chance of a man having the same type of HLA as the child in question is very low, about one in 92 (23 + 47 + 8 + 14). When HLA testing is combined with traditional ABO testing, the likelihood of parenthood can be increased or reduced even more. A general rule of thumb is that ABO testing alone can exclude the possibility that a man is the father of a child about 20 percent of the time. HLA testing can exclude the same possibility about 90 percent of the time. In combination, the two tests can exclude the possibility of parenthood by about 97 percent of all cases.

Characterization of Bloodstains

Testing for ABO group, Rh factor, human leukocyte antigens (HLA), and the like helps determine from whom a blood sample comes. Using such tests, however, is typically one of the final steps in characterizing a bloodstain. (*Characterization* of bloodstains refers to the process of identifying the stain as human or not and then recognizing other essential properties of blood in the stain, such as blood groups and polymorphic protein and isoenzymes that may be present.) Before reaching that point, a forensic scientist has to follow a number of other steps, beginning with a study of the crime scene itself.

The first step in that process is to find out if an apparent bloodstain is blood and not red paint, ketchup, or some other material. When freshly released from the body, blood has a bright red color. Within three to five minutes, however, blood begins to dry and change color, becoming dark brown or black. Wet blood is usually easier to test than dry, but, for a number of reasons, liquid samples cannot always be collected. Nor are wet samples absolutely necessary, because methods for collecting and testing dry bloodstains are now well developed.

One of the earliest tests for blood was developed in 1904 by Oskar and Rudolf Adler. The Adlers' test made use of benzidine (p-diaminodiphenyl). The benzidine test is based on the fact that blood hemoglobin behaves as if it were a peroxidase enzyme. Peroxidases are enzymes that augment the efficiency of hydrogen peroxide in oxidizing certain substrates, such as phenols or aromatic amines. When benzidine and hydrogen peroxide are added to blood, an oxidation-reduction reaction occurs in which the benzidine is converted to a product with a bluish-green color known as a diazo dye.

The Adlers' test is called a *presumptive test,* because it is based on the presumption that the material being tested is blood. Presumptive tests are quick, simple tests on evidence left at the scene of a crime to get an idea as to whether additional testing is needed. If an investigator finds a dark spot on the floor of a crime scene, the first step is to find out if the spot is blood, particularly human blood. If the spot turns out to be spilled ink or paint, no further testing is likely necessary. A presumptive test either rules out a piece of evidence as irrelevant or indicates that additional testing is necessary. The additional testing that occurs is confirmatory testing. Confirmatory testing usually takes more time, is conducted at a forensic laboratory, and provides more specific and detailed information about the object or material being tested.

In 1973, the U.S. Environmental Protection Agency banned benzidine as a suspected carcinogen. By that time, however, a variety of alternative presumptive tests for bloodstains was under development. One that has become especially popular is the Kastle-Meyer test. The Kastle-Meyer reagent is made by mixing potassium hydroxide, phenolphthalein, and zinc dust. When hydroxide peroxide and the reagent are added to blood, hemoglobin in the blood catalyzes the conversion of phenolphthalein to its deep pink configuration. Forensic scientists do not have to be concerned with the actual preparation of Kastle-Meyer reagent since it, like most other forensic chemicals, is readily available from commercial suppliers in easy-to-use kits.

Another popular presumptive test for bloodstains involves the use of Hemastix, a product of the Bayer Corporation. Hemastix are cellulose strips that contain a mixture of o-toluidine (2-methylaniline) and hydrogen peroxide. They are easy to use because one needs only to moisten the strip and dip it into the sample to be tested. If blood is present, hemoglobin catalyzes the conversion of o-toluidine to a greenish product. The intensity of the green color can be matched against a scale provided with the testing strips to determine the concentration of the blood present in the sample.

Another presumptive test for bloodstains that is based on a somewhat different principle is the luminol test, first developed by the German criminologist Walter Specht in 1937. Luminol is 5-amino-2,3-dihydro-1,4-phthalazinedione. Its structural formula is shown in the reaction in the diagram below. When treated with hydrogen peroxide in the presence of blood, one of the rings in the luminol

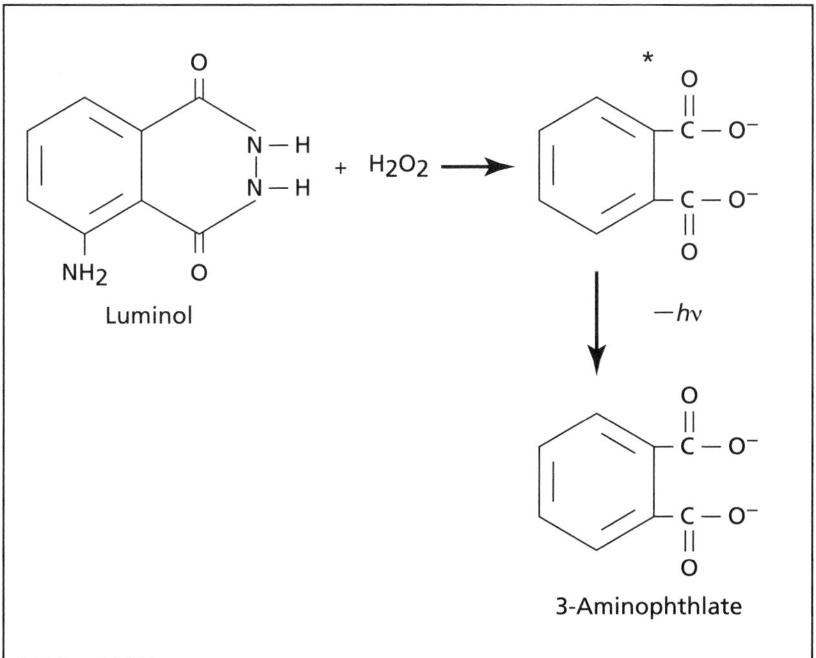

© Infobase Publishing

Luminol reaction

molecule breaks open, releasing nitrogen gas and producing a compound known as 3-aminophthlate in an excited state. In the reaction shown on page 49, the excited form of 3-aminophthlate is indicated with an asterisk. After a brief moment, 3-APA* gives off a photon with a wavelength of about 425 nanometers that corresponds to a bluish-violet light; it fluoresces.

Luminol reagent can be made "from scratch" by dissolving 5.0 grams (g) of sodium carbonate and 0.1 g of luminol in 100 milliliters of distilled water. Just before use, 0.7 g of sodium perborate is added to the sodium carbonate/luminol solution. The test is conducted in a darkened room so that the fluorescence produced by blood can be easily seen. The area to be tested is first covered with filter paper and then sprayed with a solution of household bleach. The luminol solution is then sprayed immediately on top of the bleach-soaked filter paper. If blood is present, it fluoresces with a bluish-violet color.

This fairly lengthy process is seldom used in actual practice since commercially prepared solutions of luminol are readily available. These solutions come in four-, eight-, and 16-ounce disposable spray bottles that can be used directly on suspected bloodstains.

The luminol test is popular because it is highly sensitive. It is capable of detecting bloodstains that have been diluted up to 10 million times. Luminol also produces positive tests even when a bloodstain is a few years old. It has been used to detect the presence of blood after other presumptive tests have been tried and produced negative results.

Two common confirmatory tests on bloodstains are the Takayama and Teichmann tests, both named after their inventors, the Japanese criminologist Masaeo Takayama and the Polish anatomist Ludwig Karl Teichmann (1823–95). The Teichmann test is much older, having been developed in 1853, while the Takayama test dates to 1912. In both tests, the addition of a reagent to blood results in the formation of distinctive crystals. In the Teichmann test, the reagent is a mixture of glacial acetic acid and sodium chloride. The reagent causes hemoglobin molecules to cleave, producing brownish crystals of pure hemin that have a violet, almost black, sheen. (Hemin is the form of heme that contains the Fe^{3+} ion.) In the Takayama test, pyridine is added to blood, causing the reduction of hemoglobin to a pyridine-hemoglobin complex with a characteristic salmon-pink color. In both tests, the distinctive colored crystals can easily be observed under the optical microscope.

Once a bloodstain has been confirmed, the forensic serologist must determine whether that stain has come from a human source or from some other species of animal. The test used to make this determination is called the precipitin test. The precipitin test is also known as the Ouchterlony test, after the Swedish bacteriologist Örjan Ouchterlony, who described the test in the early 1960s.

The precipitin test is based on the same antigen-antibody principle described earlier in this chapter. An experimental animal (usually a rabbit) is injected with a sample of human blood. The rabbit's blood then "recognizes" the human blood as a foreign invader and begins to manufacture antibodies to combat the human blood. Finally, blood is drawn from the rabbit. This blood now contains antibodies against human blood. If it is mixed with human blood, an antigen-antibody reaction will cause the blood mixture to agglutinate, forming a precipitate.

A variety of techniques is available for conducting this last stage of the test, including use of a capillary tube, gel diffusion, and electrophoresis. In the first method, the sample of blood to be tested and the rabbit serum can be added to a capillary tube. If the sample is human blood, a ring of precipitate (agglutinated blood) will appear between the two layers in the tube.

In the method known as gel diffusion, the blood sample and rabbit serum are placed in shallow wells in an agar gel-coated plate. Antibodies in the serum and antigens on the red blood cells have a tendency to migrate toward each other, resulting in the formation of a thin line of precipitate between the two on the test plate, as shown in the diagram on page 52. This process of diffusion of antigens and antibodies toward each other is known as immunodiffusion.

In the third version of the precipitin test, the rate of immunodiffusion is increased through the use of electrophoresis. Electrophoresis is a useful analytical technique in which one or more substances to be analyzed are deposited on a plate (usually coated with starch or agar gel). An electric potential is created across the plate by attaching a positive charge at one end of the plate and a negative charge at

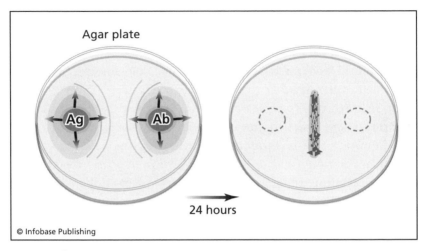

Agar plate

24 hours

© Infobase Publishing

Immunodiffusion

the opposite end of the plate. Charged particles within the sample placed on the plate then migrate to the end of the plate with the opposite charge. When antigens and antibodies are deposited on the electrophoresis plate and the charge applied, the two materials migrate toward each other, eventually forming a line of precipitin between them.

Once a blood sample has been identified as being human in origin, the last step in blood characterization is to determine its blood type or types, using the ABO, Rh, MN, and other systems described earlier. Characterization into one or more blood types is relatively simple and straightforward with samples of liquid blood, but it is somewhat more complicated with dried blood. Once blood has dried, red blood cells rupture and die. As a result, no RBCs exist with which to do standard blood-typing tests.

Alternative methods are available for use on dried blood samples, however. The two most popular are the absorption-inhibition test and the absorption-elution test. Both tests take advantage of the tendency of antibodies to attach themselves to and agglutinate with antigens. In the case of dried bloods, those antigens remain within the bloodstain even though the RBCs themselves have been destroyed.

The diagram on page 53 outlines the steps involved in conducting an absorption-inhibition test. First, the tester prepares a sample of antiserum with a known concentration of antibodies. (An antiserum is blood serum that contains antibodies.) In this example, suppose that the antiserum contains anti-A antibodies. A moistened sample of the antiserum is placed in contact with the dried blood to be tested and allowed to remain in place for a period of time. As time passes, antibodies in the antiserum will migrate to and attach themselves to any A antigens present in the dried blood. After some period of time, the antiserum is washed off the dried bloodstain and the concentration of antibodies determined by titration. The reduction in antibody concentration in the antiserum indicates whether A antigens were present in the bloodstain or not. If the concentration of antibodies

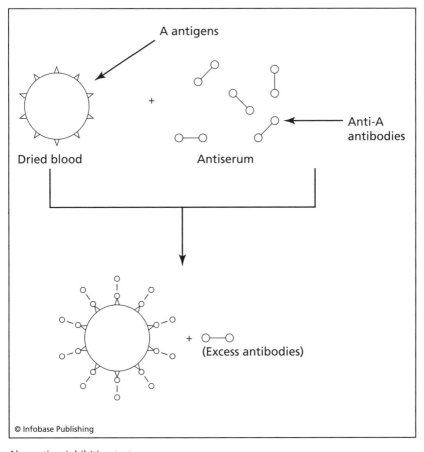

Absorption-inhibition test

was the same before and after the test, then no A antigens were present. If the concentration decreased as a result of the test's being conducted, A antigens were present and the blood can be typed.

The absorption-elution technique is conducted in much the same way as the absorption-inhibition test. Antiserum containing known antibodies (again, assume they are anti-A antibodies for this example) is allowed to remain in contact with a dried bloodstain for a period of time. Again, anti-A antibodies will bond with any A antigens present in the blood sample and remain fixed on the stain, as shown in the diagram below. Any excess antiserum is then washed off with cold water or a saline solution, and the bloodstain is heated

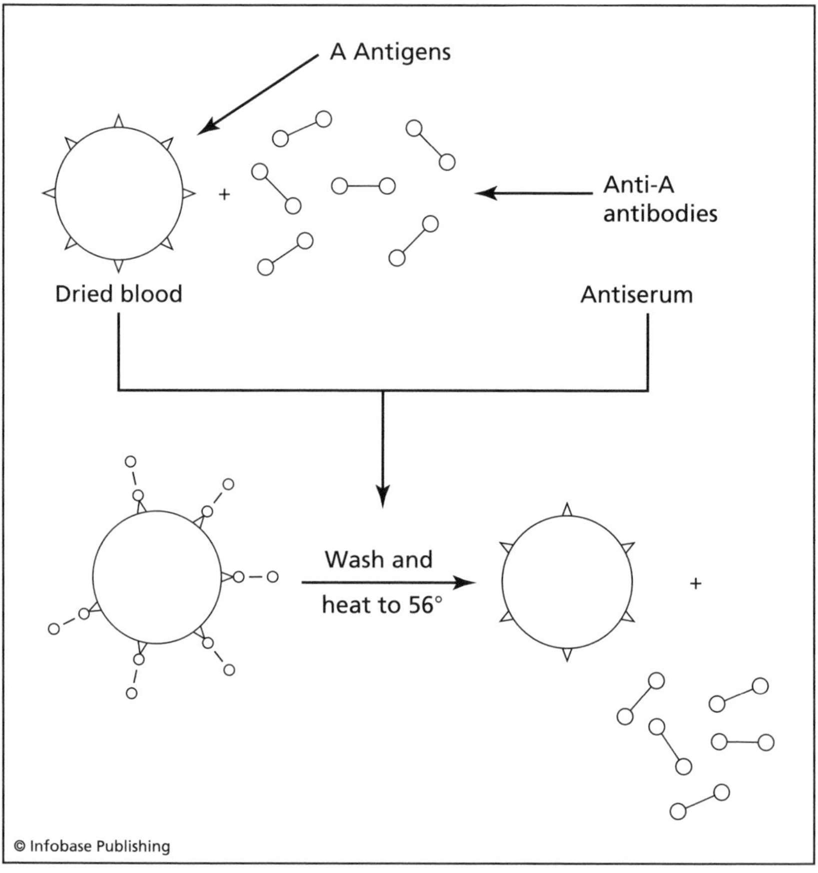

© Infobase Publishing

Absorption-elution test

to a temperature of 56°C. The removal of excess antiserum by this procedure is known as elution. If A antigens were present in the dried bloodstain, antigen-antibody bonding will occur. But heating then causes those antigen-antibody clusters to break apart, releasing free antigens and free antibodies into the washing solution. If A antigens were not present in the original bloodstain, all anti-A antibodies would have been washed off during elution.

Finally, red blood cells of some known blood type (type A would be used in this example) are added to the solution. If anti-A antibodies remain in the solution, they will agglutinate with the added blood cells, producing a visible clumping that indicates the presence of the A antigen in the original bloodstain. If no anti-A antibodies are present, no agglutination will occur, and no clumping will be observed in the solution.

The procedures described here with an antiserum containing anti-A antibodies can be repeated with anti-B antibodies. The results of these tests permit the classification of dried blood as A, B, AB, or O. Of the two tests, the absorption-elution method tends to be somewhat more sensitive, easier to conduct, and, hence, somewhat more popular. It can be used successfully on samples of blood as small as one centimeter in diameter and as old as 10 years or more.

Bloodstain Patterns

Forensic scientists have realized for more than a century that a great deal of information can be obtained, not only from the presence of blood at a crime scene and the type of blood that has been left behind, but also from the patterns in which that blood is distributed. One of the earliest works on this topic was a book published in 1895, *Origin, Shape, Direction and Distribution of the Bloodstains following Head Wounds Caused by Blows,* by Eduard Piotrowski. A decade later, one of the classics in the field of bloodstain pattern analysis (BPA) was published: *Manual for Examining Magistrate Judges, a System for Criminalists,* by the German criminologist Hans Gross (1847–1915). By the mid-20th century, forensic scientists were beginning to make extensive use of mathematics and physics in the analysis of BPA. In 1939, Victor Balthazard, professor of forensic medicine at the

Sorbonne, and his colleagues offered a paper at the 22nd Congress of Forensic Medicine in Paris on the use of geometric principles to obtain information from bloodstain patterns.

In the 21st century, the study of bloodstain patterns is a well-developed, highly sophisticated technology that can, under certain circumstances, provide extensive information about the events that occurred at a crime scene. A few of the most important elements involved in BPA studies are the types of surface on which blood falls, the shapes of the individual drops, and the shape of the overall spatter pattern.

In the first place, the type of surface on which blood falls determines to a considerable extent the type of stain formed. As the photograph on page 58 shows, the harder and smoother the surface, the more clearly defined the stain and, consequently, the more information it can provide.

The angle at which blood was projected onto a surface can also be determined from a bloodstain. If a drop of blood is dropped vertically onto a surface, for example, it tends to form a perfectly circular drop. If the blood is dropped on the surface at some angle, its shape tends to become more elliptical. The greater the angle of projection, the more elliptical the shape of the blood droplet. The angle of impact can be determined mathematically from a simple trigonometric equation:

$$\sin\alpha = \frac{w_{bloodstain}}{l_{bloodstain}}$$

where α is the angle of impact and $w_{bloodstain}$ and $l_{bloodstain}$ are the greatest width and length, respectively, of the bloodstain.

The direction taken by blood before striking a surface can also be determined from another aspect of the bloodstain's shape. Bloodstains are usually not exactly ellipsoidal in shape, but they tend to have a rounded edge at one end of the major axis and a pointed edge at the opposite end of the major axis. The pointed end of the bloodstain always faces in the direction of the blood's source.

This information can be used to reconstruct the pathway taken by blood in traveling from its source (usually the victim) to the surface on which it was found. At one time, this reconstruction was carried out with long strings, laid out on the crime scene in directions indicated by bloodstain patterns. That pattern of strings showed the source from which the blood came, the force with which it was projected, the amount of blood involved, and other factors. Today computer programs are available to carry out such reconstructions without an investigator having to lay out strings.

Further information about a crime can be obtained from spatter patterns associated with a bloodstain. For example, a low-velocity pattern may be produced if someone steps into a pool of blood, projecting it outward in a relatively cohesive amoeba-shaped array. But if the blood is projected at a greater velocity, it tends to break apart into individual droplets about one millimeter or more in diameter, forming a medium-velocity pattern. Such patterns are typical of wounds produced by relatively slow-moving blunt instruments, such as a person's fist, a hammer, knife, or baseball bat. Such weapons typically move with a velocity of less than 100 feet per second (30 m/s).

Finally, blood is broken apart into much smaller particles when it is projected by a rapidly moving object, such as a bullet fired from a gun. This configuration is called a high-velocity pattern. Except for explosions, gunshot wounds are almost invariably the cause of a high-velocity bloodstain pattern.

When all the tools of BPA are put to use, an investigator can make a number of determinations about the nature of the crime that has been committed, including:

➤ The source of the blood, that is, the place where a victim was struck in some way so as to release blood;

➤ The type of impact made that produced the blood, that is, the use of fists, a blunt instrument, a knife, or a gun;

➤ The number of incidents that occurred to produce the blood, that is, the number of gunshots or knife wounds;

➤   The direction and speed with which the victim was moving during the crime;

➤   The position of the victim during the crime; and

➤   Whether one of the victim's arteries might have been cut during the crime.

Determining blood splatter patterns is a common part of investigating a crime scene. (Mauro Fermariello/Photo Researchers, Inc.)

Sophisticated methods of blood-splatter analysis that often make use of computer programs now provide extensive and detailed information about the events that occurred at a crime scene. Evidence obtained from such studies is now widely accepted as evidence in criminal cases at local, state, and federal levels.

Testing for Semen and Saliva

Blood is only one bodily fluid used to determine the identity of a perpetrator in a crime. Two other bodily fluids that can be used for identification purposes are semen and saliva. Both fluids have special significance in certain types of crime, such as rape and sexual crime for example. Semen can be a valuable form of evidence in cases of rape; it can often be used to demonstrate that a rape has actually occurred and, in many cases, to identify the person responsible for the crime.

Characterization of semen is possible because certain components are present only in semen or are present in concentrations significantly greater than in other parts of the body. The most distinctive of these indicators, or markers, is the presence of spermatozoa.

Semen (also known as seminal fluid) is a complex mixture produced by the male reproductive organs. It contains secretions from the seminal vesicles, the prostate gland, and bulbourethral gland, the most important of which are spermatozoa, or sperm cells, the male reproductive cells. In the course of each ejaculation, the typical male produces two to five milliliters of semen containing from 100 million to 150 million sperm cells per milliliter.

Semen is typically collected at crime scenes from either of two sources. First, it may be found on some material present at the scene, such as clothing or bedding. Second, it may be obtained from the victim's body by means of a swab or washing of the vagina or rectum. The existence of semen is sometimes suggested by its appearance as a white crusty stain on an object. But the best single confirmatory test for semen is the presence of spermatozoa themselves. A suspected sample is typically moistened and examined under the microscope, sometimes with the use of a stain to make the spermatozoa more clearly visible. The detection of spermatozoa in a suspected sample is positive evidence for the existence of semen.

Although the detection of spermatozoa is a highly desirable test for semen, it is an insufficient test for a number of reasons. First, some men are aspermic, that is, incapable of producing sperm cells. For example, men who have had vasectomies are typically aspermic. Their semen is usually lacking in spermatozoa, so microscopic examination is useless in detecting the presence of semen from such men. Also, sperm tend to be relatively fragile and are easily destroyed, especially after they become dry. For these reasons, it is necessary to have additional tests for the detection of semen.

One of the most popular of such tests is the acid phosphatase test. Acid phosphatase is an enzyme that is secreted by the prostate gland. Its concentration is anywhere from 50 to 1,000 times as great in semen as in any other bodily fluid, so its presence in an unknown sample of material is suggestive of the material being semen. The test for acid phosphatase usually consists of two steps. First, the sample to be tested is sprayed with an acidic solution of sodium α-naphthyl phosphate, which is converted by acid phosphatase to α-naphthol. The α-naphthol is then detected by adding any one of a number of dyes, which produces a colored reaction with the α-naphthol. For example, the addition of a complex diazo dye known as Fast Blue B results in the formation of a deep purple color.

Interestingly enough, Japanese scientists have recently developed an over-the-counter version of the acid phosphatase test that they are marketing to women who wish to check up on their husbands' fidelity. The product, called S-check, involves a two-step process like that described above except that the second reagent reacts with α-naphthol to produce a bright green product. Acid phosphatase tests are useful in the detection of semen, at least partly because they are effective for periods of up to a few years if the material on which a stain is deposited has not been washed.

A related method for the detection of semen involves moistening the suspected sample with a compound known as 4-methyl umbelliferyl phosphate (MUP) or a derivative, 6,8-difluoro-4-methyl umbelliferyl phosphate (DiFMUP), and then exposing the moist sample to ultraviolet light. In the presence of ultraviolet light, the treated semen fluoresces with a maximum intensity between 358 and 455 nanometers in the blue region of the electromagnetic spectrum.

Another test for semen involves a protein that occurs uniquely in semen, the P30 or prostate-specific antigen (PSA) test. The test is conducted in essentially the same way as the precipitin test in the preceding section. The P30 protein is isolated from a known sample of human semen and then injected into a rabbit. The rabbit's blood produces anti-P30 antibodies, which are then extracted and used to test for P30 proteins in an unknown sample.

Two less commonly used tests are those for the detection of choline $(CH_3)_3N(OH)CH_2CH_2OH)$ and spermine $(NH_2(CH_2)_3NH(CH_2)_4$ $NH(CH_2)_3NH_2)$, both present in semen but also present in other bodily fluids. The standard test for choline (also known as the Florence test) involves the addition of elemental iodine in solution to the sample. If choline is present in the sample, it forms a complex periodide of choline that precipitates out in the form of distinctive crystals. In the test for spermine (also known as the Barberio test), a saturated solution of picric acid is added to the specimen. If spermine is present, the compound spermine picrate is formed, again in the form of crystals with a distinctive and identifiable shape. Since choline and spermine are both present in bodily fluids other than semen, the Florence and Barberio tests are both presumptive; they suggest rather than prove the presence of semen. Given the more conclusive tests for semen that are available, these tests are seldom used today.

The procedures described in this section thus far all have a single objective: to discover whether a particular stain is, in fact, human semen. Once that determination has been made, another step remains: finding out whether the semen belongs to a particular individual. That step is different for a group of individuals known as secretors and for those who are not secretors. Secretors are people whose blood type antigens also appear in their other bodily fluids. Thus, secretors have the same ABO groups in their semen as in their blood. For nonsecretors, it is often possible to use some polymorphic protein or antienzyme (such as PGM or 6-PGD) to narrow down the list of possible suspects related to the semen sample discovered.

The presence of saliva at a crime scene can sometimes be of value, although tests confirming the presence of saliva (except for

DNA testing, discussed in the next chapter) are more difficult than similar tests for blood and semen. For example, in the investigation of a suspected case of oral sex, a forensic scientist may look for the presence of saliva on the victim's body. Saliva may also be present on many other pieces of forensic evidence. For example, it may be detected in the adhesive on the stamp of a kidnap letter.

The standard method for identifying saliva has long been based on the presence of an enzyme known as amylase. The amylases are a group of enzymes produced in various parts of the body, primarily the pancreas and three pairs of salivary glands in the mouth. Their function is to break down starch molecules into smaller molecules. Starch is a glucose polysaccharide, that is, a very large *polymer* made of glucose monomers. Amylase hydrolyzes some of the α-1,4 linkages in starch, resulting in the formation of lower molecular weight glucose polysaccharides known as dextrins. Dextrins are then further hydrolyzed by amylase to form the disaccharide maltose:

$$\text{starch} \xrightarrow{\text{amylase}} \text{dextrins} \xrightarrow{\text{amylase}} \text{maltose} \xrightarrow{\text{maltase}} \text{glucose}$$

The most commonly used saliva test looks for enzymatic activity of the type shown in the equation above, in which maltose is formed.

In order to conduct the amylase test, one first moistens a filter paper or swab with a starch solution. The filter paper or swab is then pressed against the stain suspected to contain saliva. If saliva is present, the amylase it contains will hydrolyze starch on the filter paper or swab, converting it to maltose. To test for the presence of maltose, the filter paper or swab is then sprayed with a solution that detects the presence of maltose, such as Benedict's solution, Brentamine Blue, or Procion Red.

The amylase test described here is a qualitative test; that is, it indicates whether amylase is present. Since amylase is present in other bodily fluids, a preferred test is one that determines the quantity of amylase present. Since amylase occurs in a greater concentration in saliva than anywhere else in the body, a high concentration of amylase strongly suggests the presence of saliva.

Since confirmatory and characterization tests for saliva (except for ABO testing) are generally not available, a newer analytical tool,

DNA fingerprinting, is now more commonly used when information about the presence and nature of saliva is needed in a criminal investigation.

Over the past century, an impressive variety of tests has been developed to identify and characterize blood, semen, saliva, and other bodily fluids. Many of those tests are still in wide use today. They often make it possible to identify samples no more than a few nanograms in size and those that may be as much as a few years old. In many cases, the tests are sufficiently definitive to positively identify an individual as the person responsible for a crime. In spite of the effectiveness of these tests, a new and very powerful tool for discovering the relationship between forensic samples (blood and semen, for example) and one particular individual has been developed over the past two decades: DNA fingerprinting, discussed in chapter 6.

4

Toxicology and Drug Testing

Frankie and Johnny sure threw a nice party tonight! I probably shouldn't have had that last beer, but I feel OK. I can drive home without any problems. And Dad will be happy that I got in almost a half hour before my curfew. All in all, it has been an almost perfect night . . . except for the flashing lights in my rearview mirror!

So the state trooper says my car was weaving back and forth. She probably thinks I'm drunk. Well, I can walk a straight line for her. And I can pass any breath test or any other test she wants me to take. . . . I hope!

Drunk driving is one of the most serious law enforcement problems in the United States and many other parts of the world. In 2003, the last year for which data are available, 17,013 people were killed in motor vehicle accidents that involved at least one driver with a blood alcohol concentration (BAC) of 0.01 or above. Beyond drunk-driving offenses, the U.S. Bureau of Justice Statistics has estimated that in 2002 nearly half (46.6%) of all inmates in U.S. prisons and jails were either dependent on alcohol or alcohol abusers.

Determining whether a person has been using alcohol, and if so, how much, is one of the important tasks performed by forensic toxicologists. But testing for alcohol consumption is only one of many responsibilities assigned to a forensic toxicologist. These experts are also involved in determining whether a person has ingested and/or died from a poisonous substance, what that substance is, and how much was ingested. The American Academy of Forensic Sciences has defined the science of forensic toxicology as the "branch of toxicology that deals with the medico-legal aspects of toxicology." Forensic toxicologists answer the question "Did prescription or illegal drugs and/or alcohol lead or contribute to the person's death or intoxication?"

Another definition that has been suggested says that forensic toxicology deals with the relationship of the "biochemical, physiological, and pharmacological properties of drugs and poisons to the medical and legal implications associated with their used abuse or medical administration." This chapter begins with an overview of the work of a forensic toxicologist in dealing with alcohol-related problems. It then details how forensic toxicologists analyze a host of more complex substances, ranging from household cleaning supplies to opiates, cyanides, strychnine, and other poisons.

Alcohol and the Human Body

The "alcohol" in an alcoholic beverage refers to the organic chemical *ethanol,* or *ethyl alcohol.* Its chemical formula is CH_3CH_2OH. It is a colorless, volatile liquid with a pungent taste and pleasant, grapelike odor. It is completely miscible with water. Ethanol is formed during the fermentation of many organic substances, including corn, wheat, potatoes, and grapes. Ethanol is also known by a number of other names, including grain alcohol, fermentation alcohol, and spirits. Alcoholic drinks consist of alcohol mixed with water, to which may be added small amounts of other substances that add flavors and odors to the final product.

When a person ingests an alcoholic beverage, a small amount of the alcohol is absorbed by the mucous membranes that line the nose and throat, and some vaporizes into the lungs. The vast majority of

◁ **AMERICAN ACADEMY OF FORENSIC SCIENCES** ▷

In the early days of science, researchers worked essentially on their own. They often provided all the money they needed for their research projects, built the equipment they needed, taught themselves much of the knowledge they used in their work, carried out their own research, and, sometimes, paid to have the results of their work published.

But the scientific community has grown and developed a great deal over the past two centuries. Today nearly all scientists are part of a large and complex community that gives them the aid and support they need in carrying out their research and provides them with opportunities to meet and share ideas with others working in the same field. Most chemists in the United States belong to the American Chemical Society as well as to more comprehensive groups, such as the American Association for the Advancement of Science, and to more specialized groups, such as the American Association for Clinical Chemistry.

The first national organization of forensic scientists in the United States, the American Academy of Forensic Sciences (AAFS; http://www.aafs.org), was formed in 1948 to promote education in the forensic sciences and to improve accuracy, precision, and specificity in the forensic sciences. The academy today has more than 5,000 members, including physicians, attorneys, dentists, toxicologists, physical anthropologists, document examiners,

the alcohol finds its way into the stomach and small intestine, however, where it enters the bloodstream. About 20 percent of the alcohol is absorbed through the walls of the stomach, and the remainder is absorbed through the walls of the small intestine.

The presence of alcohol in the blood can be detected within minutes after a person has consumed an alcoholic beverage. Typically, blood alcohol concentration (BAC) builds rapidly, reaching a maximum an hour or two after consumption. BAC then falls off somewhat less rapidly. The pattern of BAC versus time is affected by a number of factors. For example, the presence of food in the stomach tends to decrease the amount of alcohol absorbed, although the general pattern of absorption and elimination tends to be similar. Carbonation

psychiatrists, engineers, criminalists, educators, and others who work in one forensic science field or another. Members come from all 50 of the United States and from 50 foreign countries.

One of AAFS's most important functions is to publish the *Journal of Forensic Sciences,* which contains original papers dealing with observations, scholarly inquiries, and reviews in the fields of forensic toxicology, pathology, psychiatry, immunology, jurisprudence, criminalistics, odontology, physical anthropology, and questioned documents and engineering. The academy also sponsors a number of meetings, including its annual meeting, meetings on specialized topics, and educational forums.

Much of the academy's work is carried out through its special-interest sections, which include criminalistics, engineering sciences, jurisprudence, odontology, pathology and biology, physical anthropology, psychiatry and behavioral sciences, questioned documents, toxicology, and general interest.

The academy also sponsors and supports the Young Forensic Scientists Forum (YFSF), a group dedicated to the education and development of young forensic scientists. YFSF sponsors a number of activities for its members, including a regular newsletter, a mentoring program, access to Internet resources, and answers to questions in the field of forensic science.

---

also affects the rate at which alcohol in a drink is absorbed. The presence of bubbles tends to increase the rate at which alcohol is absorbed, meaning, for example, that alcohol in a glass of champagne tends to enter the bloodstream more rapidly than alcohol from a glass of wine.

The body eventually eliminates between 95 and 98 percent of the alcohol consumed in an alcoholic beverage by two processes: oxidation and excretion. Oxidation takes place in the liver, where the enzyme alcohol dehydrogenase, in conjunction with the coenzyme nicotinamide adenine dinucleotide (NAD), converts ethanol first to acetaldehyde, then to acetic acid, and eventually to carbon dioxide and water:

(1) CH_3CH_2OH $\xrightarrow{\text{alcohol dehydrogenase + NAD}}$ CH_3CHO

(2) CH_3CHO $\xrightarrow{\text{acetaldehyde dehydrogenase + NAD}}$ CH_3COOH

(3) $CH_3COOH \rightarrow CO_2 + H_2O$

The metabolism of alcohol differs significantly from that of other drugs. In most cases, increasing the amount of a drug in the bloodstream increases the rate at which it is metabolized. In the case of alcohol, the rate of metabolism is independent of its concentration in the bloodstream. If a person continues to drink alcoholic beverages over a period of time, it results in a constantly increasing level of blood alcohol concentration, with no increase in the rate of metabolism. That rate averages about 0.3 ounce ([oz.]; 10 milliliters [mL]) of pure (100 percent) ethanol per hour, which is equivalent to about 1 oz. (25 mL) of a "hard" alcoholic beverage, such as whiskey (about 40 percent ethanol); about 3 oz. (80 mL) of wine (about 12 percent ethanol); or about 7 oz. (200 mL) of beer (about 5 percent ethanol).

These data provide guidelines for relatively safe drinking. If a person limits alcohol intake to 1 oz. of "hard" liquor per hour (or an equivalent amount of beer or wine), the body will be able to metabolize most of the ethanol ingested without any buildup in the bloodstream. If one consumes alcohol at a faster rate, it will continue to accumulate in the bloodstream, resulting in increasing levels of intoxication.

Once alcohol reaches the bloodstream, it is carried to all parts of the body and absorbed by cells throughout the body, where it produces its pharmacological effects. Pharmacological effects are changes caused by drugs on the physiology and behavior of an organism. Alcohol has a great effect on the central nervous system, where the compound acts as a general, nonselective depressant, that is, it slows down the function of neurons within the brain. The increasingly severe effects of this depressive action are summarized in the chart on pages 69–70, which shows the effects of various blood alcohol concentrations on a person's behavior.

◄ BEHAVIORAL EFFECTS OF VARYING LEVELS OF BLOOD ALCOHOL CONCENTRATION (BAC) ►

BAC*	STATE	CHARACTERISTICS
0.03–0.12	Euphoria	Increased sociability, talkativeness, self-confidence; decreased inhibition; loss of judgment, control, and attention; some loss of sensory-motor function; decreased efficiency in performance tests
0.09–0.25	Excitement	Emotional instability; loss of critical judgment; drowsiness; further loss of sensory-motor function and coordination; decreased re-action time; impaired perception, memory, and comprehension; reduced visual acuity and peripheral vision
0.18–0.30	Confusion	Disorientation, mental confusion, dizziness, exaggerated emotional states, increased threshold for pain, staggering, slurred speech, apathy, and lethargy

(continues)

◁ **BEHAVIORAL EFFECTS OF VARYING LEVELS OF BLOOD ALCOHOL CONCENTRATION (BAC)** *(continued)* ▷

BAC*	STATE	CHARACTERISTICS
0.25–0.40	Stupor	Inability to stand or walk, vomiting, incontinence, sleepiness, lack of response to stimuli, loss of most motor functions, impaired consciousness, and inertia
0.35–0.50	Coma	Complete unconsciousness, depressed body temperature, incontinence, impairment of circulatory and respiratory functions, depressed or abolished reflexes, and possible death
>0.45	Death	Death from respiratory arrest

*Parts alcohol per 1,000 parts of blood

Testing for Blood Alcohol Concentration

Blood alcohol concentration (BAC) became a matter of concern to forensic scientists in the mid-1930s. On December 5, 1933, the Eighteenth Amendment to the United States Constitution, prohibiting the manufacture, sale, and transportation of alcoholic beverages in the United States, was repealed. It once again became legal for U.S. citizens to buy and use alcoholic beverages. With the repeal of the Eighteenth Amendment, law enforcement officials were confronted with a variety of problems related to the misuse of alcoholic beverages.

In March 1939, Indiana became the first state to adopt legislation permitting police to stop motorists suspected of being under the influence of alcohol and to conduct tests to determine motorists' BAC. A month later, Maine passed similar legislation. The question both laws raised was how one would determine a person's BAC. To be strictly accurate, the only way to determine how a person's behavior (such as the ability to drive) was being affected by alcohol would be to draw a blood sample from a person's brain and determine the BAC of that sample. Such a procedure is obviously impossible to implement for at least two reasons. First, the procedure would be far too risky for the benefits achieved. And second, there would be no way to conduct such tests "on the spot," that is, on a highway or road where a motorist with suspicious driving patterns could be tested.

Forensic scientists realized early on, however, that alternative methods of testing for BAC were possible. Probably the first of these alternative methods to be adopted involved the testing of a person's breath for alcohol. The BAC of a person's breath is not identical with the BAC of his or her blood, but it is an accurate enough reflection of BAC to be a useful measure of a person's level of inebriation.

The first device for measuring the BAC of a person's breath was the Drunkometer, invented by Rolla Harger, professor of biochemistry at Indiana University. The Drunkometer consisted of a balloon into which a person exhaled. The air in the balloon was then released into a chemical solution that changed color in proportion to the amount of alcohol present in the balloon (and, hence, the person's breath).

The reaction on which the Drunkometer was based, in which ethanol reacts with and reduces potassium permanganate ($KMnO_4$), is one familiar to many high school students. A deeply purple permanganate solution gradually loses its color as more ethanol is added to it. A series of reactions occurs during this change, one of which is the following:

$$3CH_3CH_2OH + KMnO_4 \rightarrow 3CH_3CH_2O + MnO_2 + KOH + H_2O$$

A device similar to the Drunkometer, called the Intoximeter, operated on a similar principle. The operation of a third device, called the Alcometer, was based on a similar oxidation-reduction reaction between ethanol and iodine pentoxide (I_2O_5). In this case, the oxidizing agent is diiodine pentoxide (I_2O_5), which oxidizes ethanol and is itself reduced to elemental iodine:

$$I_2O_5 + 10CH_3CH_2OH \rightarrow I_2 + 10CH_3CH_2O + 5H_2O$$

The elemental iodine that forms has a pale brown color, contrasting with the colorless diiodine pentoxide from which it is formed. The intensity of the color increases as more ethanol is present to react with the diiodine pentoxide. The color change can be made even more pronounced by adding starch to the solution. Iodine reacts with starch to give a pronounced and characteristic blue color whose intensity, again, varies with the concentration of ethanol present.

Ethanol-detecting instruments with the names Intoximeter and Alcometer are still available for sale. They no longer operate on the chemical principles just described, however, but on newer and more accurate reactions that will be described later in this chapter.

In any case, the Drunkometer, Intoximeter, and Alcometer were all soon displaced by another invention, the Breathalyzer, invented in 1954 by Robert Borkenstein (1912–2002), then of the Indiana State Police and later chairman of Indiana University's new Department of Police Administration. In the Breathalyzer test, a subject is asked to breathe into a container, whose contents are then emptied into a chamber containing potassium dichromate ($K_2Cr_2O_7$), sulfuric acid (H_2SO_4), and silver nitrate ($AgNO_3$). The reaction that occurs is primarily between ethanol in the sample that has been collected and potassium dichromate, with sulfuric acid providing hydrogen ions necessary for the reaction and silver nitrate acting as a catalyst. The reaction that occurs is as follows:

$$\overset{AgNO_3}{3CH_3CH_2OH + 2K_2Cr_2O_7 + 8H_2SO_4 \rightarrow}$$
$$2Cr_2(SO_4)_3 + 2K_2SO_4 + 3CH_3COOH + 11H_2O$$

The key change that takes place occurs when the reddish-orange dichromate ion is converted to the greenish chromium(III) ion. The greater the amount of ethanol present, the more complete the conversion of dichromate to chromium(III).

This conversion can be seen easily with the naked eye, but the amount of change cannot be judged reliably by visual means only. Instead, the reaction chamber is exposed to a photometric analysis that determines the pattern of wavelengths present in the final solution, indicating the extent to which conversion of the chromium has occurred. This analysis can be converted into an electric signal that can be read easily on a dial, indicating the subject's BAC.

Breath-testing devices were widely used in the United States from the early 1940s until the 1990s. Such devices were subject to a number of errors, however, many of them resulting from incorrect operator use. As a consequence, the devices were largely replaced by other types of analytical devices, primarily infrared spectroscopic and fuel cell devices.

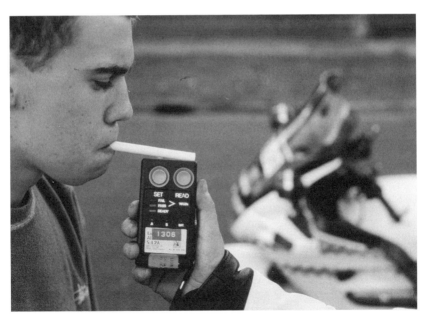

A motorist suspected of driving under the influence of alcohol takes a Breathalyzer test at the side of the road. (Jim Varney/Photo Researchers, Inc.)

◄ ROBERT BORKENSTEIN (1912–2002) ►

Drinking and driving are a deadly combination. Every forensic scientist, every law enforcement officer, and most average citizens recognize that fact. But just knowing that fact does not necessarily make it any easier for law enforcement officials to prevent people who have had too much to drink from driving and becoming involved in accidents. Those officials also need tools to let them know *how much* a particular person has had to drink and *how likely* it is that that person will become involved in an accident.

Few people in the history of forensic science have contributed more to both of these questions than Robert Borkenstein. Borkenstein was born in Fort Wayne, Indiana, on August 31, 1912. He had a relatively modest early education that ended when he graduated from high school in 1930. After a series of jobs, he was hired as a photographer by the Indiana State Police in 1936. Borkenstein soon discovered that police work was the career in which he was most interested, and he remained with the state police for 22 more years. He was eventually appointed director of the state crime lab, and he retired from the state police with the title of captain in 1958.

Late in his law enforcement career, Borkenstein decided that he wanted to earn a college degree, and he enrolled at Indiana University, where he majored in forensic science. He received his bachelor's degree in that field in 1958 and was immediately made professor and chair of the Department of Police Science at Indiana. He remained in this post until his retirement in 1983.

Long before he had earned his college degree, Borkenstein had begun to make important contributions to the field of forensic chemistry. In 1938, he and Rolla Harger, a friend at Indiana University, invented the Drunkometer, a simple device for measuring blood alcohol concentration (BAC). Although

The most widely used forms of breath alcohol testing in use today are based on spectroscopic techniques. The diagram on page 76 illustrates the general principles involved in spectroscopic analysis. A sample to be examined is inserted into a container, (1) in the diagram. A light source (2) emits a beam of light that passes through the chamber and exits at the opposite end (3). The exiting light is then passed through filters (4) that separate the light into its components and is transmitted to a photodetector (5) that measures the

the invention broke new ground in attempts to measure a person's BAC, the device was clumsy and unreliable. Sixteen years later, Borkenstein produced an improved model of the Drunkometer, the Breathalyzer, which quickly became a valuable field assessment tool for police officers.

Shortly after joining the Indiana faculty, Borkenstein began to plan the first epidemiological study on the effects of BAC on the likelihood of one's becoming involved in an automobile accident. He and his colleagues studied 5,985 drivers in Grand Rapids, Michigan, who had been involved in accidents during 1962–63. The study results suggested a driver with a BAC of 0.08 percent was twice as likely to have a crash as one with a BAC of 0.05 percent. Borkenstein's study had a number of important limitations, but it is widely recognized as the first piece of scientific research on which DUI (driving under the influence [of alcohol]) laws could be based.

Borkenstein was involved in a number of forensic and traffic organizations throughout his life. He attended the first meeting of the International Council on Alcohol, Drugs, and Traffic Safety in 1950 and, according to an obituary in the council's newsletter, "provided the leadership and inspiration for organizing its international meetings through the next four decades." He was awarded an honorary Doctor of Science degree from Wittenberg University in Springfield, Ohio, in 1963 and an honorary Doctor of Laws degree from Indiana University in 1987. He was also recognized by a number of honors and awards, including the Liberty Bell Award of the Indiana Bar Association in 1966, a special citation from the Republic of China in 1970, and the Widmark Award of the International Council on Alcohol, Drugs, and Traffic Safety in 1981. He was the author of more than 45 articles in the field of forensic science and traffic safety. Borkenstein died in Bloomington, Indiana, on August 10, 2002.

amount of light received at each wavelength. The pattern produced by the photodetector is then converted by a microprocessor (6) into an electric signal, which can be read directly by an operator.

The physical principle involved in the operation of the spectrometer is that each atom, molecule, ion, or free radical absorbs energy from the incident light in a unique way. Each particle (atom, molecule, ion, or free radical) uses that energy to change its rate of vibration, molecular rotation, or electronic state. Since the bond

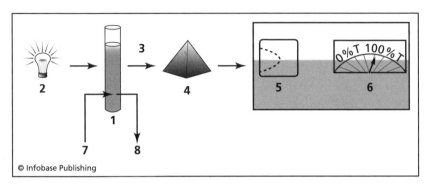

© Infobase Publishing

Principle of spectrophotometry

structures in all chemical species differ from each other in unique ways, the amount of energy they will absorb at various wavelengths will also be different. That is, the absorption spectrum obtained by this device serves as a distinctive fingerprint by which any particular chemical species can be identified.

The only adaptation needed to use the device (explained in the diagram above) as a breath alcohol analyzer is to add portals through which air can enter and exit. The subject is asked to breathe into one portal (7). That air then exits through a second portal (8). Any alcohol in the subject's breath is retained in the chamber. When light passes through the chamber, that alcohol will absorb wavelengths in its own pattern, a pattern that can then be detected at the microprocessor. The intensity of the pattern can also be measured, indicating the concentration of ethanol present in the subject's breath.

The type of light source used in spectrometric methods is very important. The spectrograms obtained by using visual light and light of longer wavelengths (in the ultraviolet region) tend to be fairly simple and often quite similar for different chemical species. Spectrograms obtained using infrared light, however, are much more complex and reliably unique. The diagram on page 77, for example, shows the spectrograms obtained for aspirin using both infrared light (at the left) and ultraviolet light (at the right). Clearly, the infrared spectrogram is far more useful in identifying the product than the ultraviolet spectrogram because it has more detail.

Another device that has been developed for testing a subject's BAC is based on the fuel cell, a device for converting chemical energy directly into electrical energy. The diagram on page 78 shows how a fuel cell can be adapted for use as a BAC testing device. The fuel cell contains two electrodes separated from each other by an electrolyte. The electrodes are typically made of platinum metal, and the electrolyte is normally sulfuric acid. The fuel cell casing consists of a porous material that allows air to pass into and out of the container. A subject is asked to breathe into a tube that carries air from his or her mouth into the fuel cell. Any alcohol in the subject's breath will be oxidized at the anode of the fuel cell to yield acetic acid (CH_3CH_2COOH), hydrogen ions (H^+), and electrons (e^-). The electrons travel to the cathode, where they are routed through an electrical meter before they return to the electrolyte. The hydrogen ions combine with atmospheric oxygen and excess electrons to form water. And the acetic acid becomes part of the electrolyte.

The subject's BAC is measured by recording the amount of current that flows through the fuel cell. The more alcohol he or she breathes into the device, the greater the amount of oxidation that will occur, the greater the number of electrons that will be formed, and the stronger the electrical current that will be produced. The number

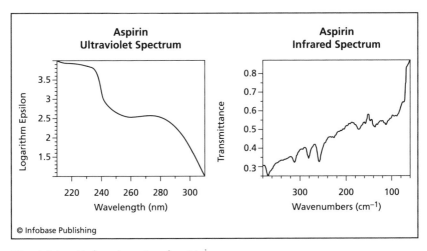

Ultraviolet and infrared spectra of aspirin

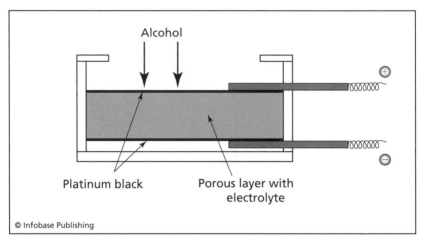

© Infobase Publishing

Fuel cell used as a breath analyzer

of electrons passing through the electrical meter is registered by a microprocessor and converted to a readable output.

The fuel cell is widely regarded as one of the most reliable devices for measuring BAC and one of the easiest such devices for law enforcement officers to use, especially for on-site testing of subjects. Wider use is limited, to some extent, by its high price, ranging from about $400 to $700 per unit.

Another form of BAC testing device has been developed, partly in the hope that individuals themselves may be interested in their own blood alcohol levels. These consumer-oriented devices are small, relatively simple, less expensive, and considerably less accurate than devices used by law enforcement officials. But they do provide the user with a general idea as to his or her BAC, perhaps encouraging a more cautious approach to drinking and/or driving.

One such device looks something like a cellular telephone, except smaller. To test one's BAC, the user must turn on the device and allow a battery to heat up a small metal coil within the casing. The coil is embedded in a sensing element made of a semiconductor, most frequently consisting of tin oxide (SnO_2). When the person's breath passes over the heated coil, alcohol molecules lose electrons to the coil. The additional electrons change the resistance of the coil, a change that can be detected by the semiconductor. The semiconductor converts the change in resistance of the coil to an equivalent BAC level that is then displayed on a screen. Devices of this design are now available for as little as about $50.

A number of devices have been developed for testing the alcohol concentration in a person's saliva. The alcohol concentration found in saliva is not identical to that found in blood or breath, but it is close enough to measure a person's sobriety. In a saliva test, a cotton swab is passed around the inside of a person's mouth and under the tongue until the swab is thoroughly moistened. The swab is then brought into contact with a test surface that changes color if alcohol is present. The degree of color change, again, is a direct indication of the amount of alcohol in the person's saliva and can be displayed as a number, such as 0.02 or 0.05.

One system used as a detector for the test surface consists of two enzymes, alcohol oxidase and peroxidase, and color indicator 3,3',5,5'-tetramethylbenzidine (TMB). If alcohol is added to this system, it is oxidized by the alcohol oxidase, forming an aldehyde and hydrogen peroxide (H_2O_2):

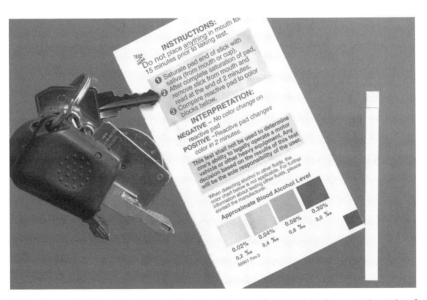

A simple test for blood alcohol level involves the use of a test stick, shown at the right of this photograph, that is inserted into one's mouth. (Voisin/Photo Researchers, Inc.)

$$CH_3CH_2OH + O_2 \xrightarrow{\text{alcohol oxidase}} CH_3CH_2O + H_2O_2$$

The hydrogen peroxide formed in this reaction then reacts with TMB to form a colored product, whose intensity of color is directly related to the amount of alcohol in the sample being tested:

$$H_2O_2 + TMB \xrightarrow{\text{peroxidase}} \text{colored product}$$

Scientific studies suggest that saliva tests for BAC are about as accurate as other measurements based on breath analyzers.

Blood alcohol concentration can also be measured by taking a sample of a person's blood and then testing it by a variety of means to determine the amount of alcohol present in the sample. The most reliable and most commonly used method for testing BAC by this direct approach is by means of a combination of *gas chromatography* and mass spectrometry, a technique described in the next section.

Like other forensic tests, BAC measurements are always subject to some question because of personal errors, problems with equipment, and other factors. Overall, however, BAC measuring devices are regarded as highly reliable when operated properly by trained personnel, and evidence obtained from such devices is routinely accepted in most courts of law as sufficient evidence for a guilty finding in a driving under the influence case or a similar alcohol-related crime.

Testing for Drugs

Although alcohol testing is an important part of the work of the modern forensic toxicologist, a specialist in that field is also called upon to test for a wide variety of other substances that fall into two general categories: poisons and illegal drugs. Well over 10,000 different poisons are known, but only a small number of these substances are likely to be involved in some kind of criminal activity with which a forensic toxicologist has to deal. Examples of those poisons include arsenic, strychnine, atropine, and cyanide.

Cocaine hydrochloride has a characteristic crystalline structure. (Leonard Lessin/Photo Researchers, Inc.)

Testing for illegal drugs has become an increasingly important part of the forensic toxicologist's job description over the past few decades. According to the 2005 National Survey on Drug Use and Health produced by the Substance Abuse and Mental Health Service Administration, 19.7 million Americans over the age of 12 had reported using an illicit drug during the previous month. Marijuana and hashish were by far the most popular illegal drugs, with 14.6 million Americans reporting that they had used the drugs in the preceding month. The next most popular illicit drugs were cocaine (2.4 million individuals); hallucinogens, such as LSD, PCP, and ecstasy (1.1 million individuals); and heroin (136,000 individuals). About 3.6 million Americans were classified as being dependent on an illegal substance or as abusing that substance on a regular basis.

Drug abuse is a matter of concern to forensic toxicologists because such acts are in and of themselves illegal. Beyond that, however, drug use is often closely related to violent and nonviolent crime. In its 2001 annual report, for example, the National Institute of Justice reported that about 6.3 percent of all Americans reported using illegal drugs, whereas about 65 percent of all criminal offenders used illegal drugs. Obviously, the link between drug abuse and criminal activity is strong.

In addition, one of the primary techniques now being used to control and reduce the problem of drug abuse in the United States is the use of drug-testing programs by business and industry. In its 2001 survey of medical-testing practices in companies, the American Management Association found that 68 percent of the 1,627 firms that responded to its survey reported using drug testing of its current employees and/or of all applications for employment.

Tests for drugs and poisons tend to fall into two categories: screening and confirmation. A screening test is generally performed first on a sample to be identified. The purpose of the test is to "weed out" a large number of drugs or poisons from consideration. Such tests identify the general class of substances to which the sample may belong, but they do not give a unique and specific characterization. A special type of screening test that is frequently used is a presumptive test. A presumptive test is one that is carried out when an investigator has enough reason to believe that a particular substance is present in a sample; that is, its presence is presumed.

Screening and presumptive tests are only the first step in determining the identity of some unknown substance, however. A second type of test, a confirmatory test, must always be carried out following the screening or presumptive test in an effort to identify the specific and unique chemical identity of the substance present in the sample being studied.

Over the years, a number of chemical tests have been developed as screening tests for certain drugs. These tests are not necessarily specific for the drugs involved since, in many cases, they can produce a *false-positive*. A false-positive is a test result that suggests that a particular substance is present in a sample when it is really not. A comparable result known as a *false-negative* is also sometimes obtained. A false negative is a test result that suggests that a particular substance is absent from a sample when it is actually present. Since false-positives and false-negatives are not unusual in screening tests, confirmatory tests are usually necessary to determine whether a suspected substance is actually present in a sample.

Some commonly used chemical color tests for drugs are the Marquis test, the Mandelin test, the Scott test, the Dille-Koppanyi test, the Duquenois-Levine test, and the Van Urk (or Ehrlich's) test. All color tests like these are used for screening purposes only and never as confirmatory tests.

The Marquis test has been known since at least 1896. It provides useful results primarily with two classes of organic compounds, the opiates and the amphetamines. Opiates are natural or synthetic drugs whose effects on the body are similar to those produced by morphine, a natural product obtained from the opium poppy, *Papaver sominferum*. These effects include difficulty in breathing, swelling of the lips and tongue, seizures, clamminess, dizziness, severe weakness, and unconsciousness. Some of the most familiar opiates are morphine itself; its natural derivatives (codeine and heroin); and the synthetic and semisynthetic derivates of morphine, meperidine (Demerol), and methadone (Dolophine). The amphetamines are a family of synthetic compounds derived from the neurotransmitter epinephrine (adrenaline). Like the natural compound on which they are based, amphetamines stimulate the central nervous system (CNS), producing "highs" that make them popular as recreational drugs. Some common examples of amphetamines are benzedrine ("bennies" or "uppers"), dexedrine ("dexies"), methedrine ("crank," "crystal," "ice," "splash," or "speed"), and a group of compounds synthesized from the amphetamine methylenedioxyamphetamine (MDA), all the members of which are known as "ecstasy." Some members of the ecstasy group are 4-bromo-2,5-dimethoxyamphetamine (DOB); N-methyl-1-(1,3-benzodioxol-5-yl)-2-aminobutane (MBDB); 3,4-methylenedioxyethamphetamine (MDE); and the most widely sold form of ecstasy, methylenedioxymethamphetamine (MDMA).

The Marquis reagent consists of a mixture of formaldehyde and sulfuric acid in a ratio that differs somewhat from test to test. Most commonly, the concentration of formaldehyde ranges from about 2 to 5 percent. A drop or two of the reagent is placed on the sample to be tested, and any color changes that occur are noted. With the opiates, the reagent gives a purple color that differs somewhat in hue and intensity depending on the specific opiate present. With amphetamines, the reagent turns orangish-brown, with similar

◄ COLOR CHANGES FOR MARQUIS REAGENT WITH SELECTED DRUGS ▷

DRUG	COLOR CHANGE
2C-C (2,5-dimethyoxy-4-chlorophenethylamine)	Lime green
2C-T-4 (2,5-dimethoxy-4-(i)-propylthiophenethylamine)	Orange to red
AMT (α-methyltryptamine)	Dark brownish-yellow
DPT (N,N-dipropyltryptamine)	Dirty olive
MBDB (2-methylamino-1-(3,4-methylenedioxyphenyl) butane)	Dark brown to black
PMA (p-methoxyamphet-amine)	No color change
Yohimibine	Slight fizzing, turning olive green

Source: Adapted from "Ecstasy Testing Kit FAQ," http://www.erowid.org/chemicals/mdma/mdma_faq_testing_kits.shtml

variations because of the specific chemical present. The chart above shows the characteristic reaction of the Marquis reagent with selected examples of other, less well-known drugs.

As with nearly all color tests, forensic chemists are generally not familiar with the specific chemical reactions by which such color changes occur. Such changes are often complex, with mechanisms that have not yet been determined.

Mandelin reagent is a solution that can be used to test for a somewhat wider variety of drugs known as alkaloids. The alkaloids are a large class of naturally occurring compounds with complex structures that usually include a heterocyclic nitrogen-containing ring. Some familiar alkaloids include atrophine, codeine, caffeine, cocaine, heroin, morphine, nicotine, quinine, and strychnine. Mandelin reagent consists of a 1 percent solution of ammonium vandanate (NH_4VO_3) in concentrated sulfuric acid. Various alkaloids produce characteristic color changes when treated with Mandelin reagent. For example, cocaine turns orange; codeine, olive; and heroin, brown.

Cobalt(II) thiocyanate ($Co(CNS)_2$) is widely used as a test for cocaine, an analysis generally known as the Scott test. The test can be used for the two forms in which cocaine is typically available, "crack" or "free base" cocaine—in which the compound exists as a basic substance—and cocaine hydrochloride—a form in which the substance has been converted to an acidified powdered form. This

Crack cocaine is prepared by mixing ammonia with a solution of cocaine hydrochloride, producing rocklike lumps of nearly pure cocaine. (TEK Image/Photo Researchers, Inc.)

difference is of some practical significance because the legal penalties for the possession of crack cocaine are generally more severe than those for possession of cocaine hydrochloride.

To perform the Scott test, a tester adds a few drops of a 2 percent solution of cobalt(II) thiocyanate and a small amount of chloroform to a small sample suspected of containing cocaine. The chloroform is needed to dissolve any cocaine that may be present. If cocaine hydrochloride is present in the sample, a blue precipitate will form. If crack cocaine is present, there will be no color change. The presence of cocaine in its basic form can be detected, however, by adding to this mixture a drop or two of any strong acid, such as nitric or sulfuric acid. The acid converts the basic crack cocaine to its acidified form, which then forms a blue precipitate with the cobalt(II) thiocyanate.

The Dille-Koppanyi test is commonly used as a presumptive test for barbiturates. Barbiturates are depressants that are derivatives of the heterocyclic compound barbituric acid $(C_4H_4N_2O_3)$. Some commonly used barbiturates include phenobarbital (a tranquilizer), pentobarbital sodium (Nembutal, a sleeping pill), the sedatives secobarbital (Seconal) and amobarbital (amytal), and sodium pentothal (an anesthetic). The Dille-Koppanyi reagent consists of two solutions. Solution A consists of a 0.1 percent solution of cobalt acetate $(Co(C_2H_3O_2)_2)$ dissolved in methanol or isopropanol to which has been added a few drops of glacial acetic acid $(HC_2H_3O_2)$. Solution B consists of a 5 percent solution of isopropylamine (2-aminopropane; $(CH_3)_2CHNH_2$) dissolved in methane. Two parts of solution A are added to the sample being tested, followed by the addition of one part of solution B. If a barbiturate is present in the sample, the mixture turns violet blue.

A widely used presumptive test for marijuana is the Duquenois-Levine test. The Duquenois-Levine reagent consists of three parts. Solution A is a mixture of 1 percent acetaldehyde (CH_3CHO) and 2 percent vanillin $[(CH_3O)(OH)C_6H_3CHO]$ in ethanol. Solution B consists of concentrated hydrochloric acid, and Solution C is pure chloroform. When the three solutions are added to the sample being tested, multiple layers are formed, the most dense of which is the chloroform layer. If that layer develops a purple color, marijuana

◀ SOME SELECTED MICROCRYSTALLINE TEST RESULTS ▷

DRUG	REAGENT	TEST RESULTS
Codeine	$HgI_2 + KI$	Small, yellowish spheres
Heroin	$HgCl_2$	Fine dendritic crystals
Methadone	I-KI	Small colorless to white needles
Methamphetamine	$HAuBr_4$	Irregular orangish-brown blades to needles
Morphine	K_2HgI_4	Brownish brushes, fans, or rosettes
Quinine	H_2PtBr_6	Orange plate-shaped crystals

Sources: Adapted from "Microchemical Identification of Some Modern Analgesics." United Nations Office on Drugs and Crime, Bulletin 1959-01. Available online. URL: http://www.unodc.org/unodc/en/bulletin/bulletin_1959-01-01_1_page005.html; "Micro-identification of the Opium Alkaloids." United Nations Office on Drugs and Crime, Bulletin 1955-01. Available online. URL: http://www.unodc.org/unodc/en/bulletin/bulletin_1955-01-01_3_page005.html.

may be present in the sample. But this test, like other presumptive tests, is not specific for marijuana; it produces similar results with a variety of vegetative materials.

A popular test for LSD (lysergic acid diethylamide) makes use of the Van Urk reagent, sometimes referred to as Ehrlich's reagent. LSD is a moderately popular recreational drug with hallucinatory effects that can become habit-forming and may result in serious long-term physical and psychological effects. The Van Urk reagent consists of a 1–2 percent solution of p-dimethylaminobenzaldehyde (p-$(CH_3)_2NC_6H_4CHO$) dissolved in equal parts concentrated hydrochloric acid and absolute (95 percent) ethanol. When LSD is added to this solution, it turns bluish purple. The Van Urk reagent also gives characteristic results with certain other hallucinogenic drugs, such as psilocin (bluish gray) and psilocybin (reddish brown), both components of certain species of mushrooms that produce hallucinogenic effects.

Although color tests can be helpful as presumptive tests for a variety of drugs, they tend to be nonspecific. A more precise test for such drugs is based on their crystalline structure. When a particular drug is treated with a few drops of a specific reagent, small crystals with characteristic shapes are formed. These microcrystals can be examined under a microscope and compared with recorded images from libraries that contain hundreds of such crystalline patterns. For example, when a 10 percent aqueous solution of sodium acetate ($NaC_2H_3O_2$) is added to heroin, crystals with the shape of hexagonal plates are formed. The same solution added to quinine, by contrast, produces crystals with irregular, log-shaped crystals. The chart on page 87 lists the types of results that are obtained for certain drugs with certain reagents. These results are highly dependent on the conditions under which the tests are carried out.

Color tests and microcrystalline tests are useful screening tests in determining the likelihood that some given substance is a drug. When positive results are obtained from such tests, confirmatory tests are necessary to obtain positive identification of a substance.

Testing for Poisons

Testing for poisons is somewhat more daunting than testing for drugs. At least 10,000 toxic substances (poisons) are known. A forensic toxicologist, however, is likely to encounter only a small fraction of that number.

Poisons are often divided into two general categories: inorganic substances and organic substances. Some examples of inorganic poisons are the compounds of metals and semimetals such as antimony, arsenic, barium, cadmium, copper, and iron. Some common organic poisons are the carbamate pesticides, digoxin and digitoxin, the organophosphorus pesticides, nicotine, and strychnine. The IPCSINTOX database published by the International Programme on Chemical Safety of the United Nations Environment Programme lists 113 different poisons with methods for testing that are, in most cases, unique to the specific poison. The number of different poisons and the specificity of tests makes it impractical to describe the testing of poisons in this book. One example, the Forrest test for imipramine, however, illustrates the approach that is used in many cases.

Forrest reagent is used to test for the presence of imipramine, a tricyclic organic compound widely used as an antidepressant. Forrest reagent is made by mixing 25 milliliters (mL) of a 2 percent aqueous solution of potassium dichromate ($K_2Cr_2O_7$) with equal volumes of concentrated sulfuric acid, concentrated perchloric acid ($HClO_4$), and concentrated nitric acid. The Forrest test is conducted by adding 1 mL of this reagent to 0.5 mL of urine, then stirring the mixture for five seconds. In a positive result, the solution turns a yellowish-green hue that slowly deepens to give a dark green through blue color. The test, like most tests described in the IPCSINTOX document, is a presumptive test, since similar results are obtained by compounds related to imipramine, such as desipramine, trimipramine, and clomipramine. A positive result with the Forrest reagent is followed, therefore, by a confirmatory test, such as a gas chromatography/ mass spectrometry test, described in the next section.

Confirmatory Tests

Only a few tests can provide unequivocal evidence of the presence of a specific chemical compound in a test sample. One of those methods, infrared spectrophotometry, was already discussed in the section on alcohol testing. The spectral patterns obtained for various chemical compounds are essentially unique, and they can be

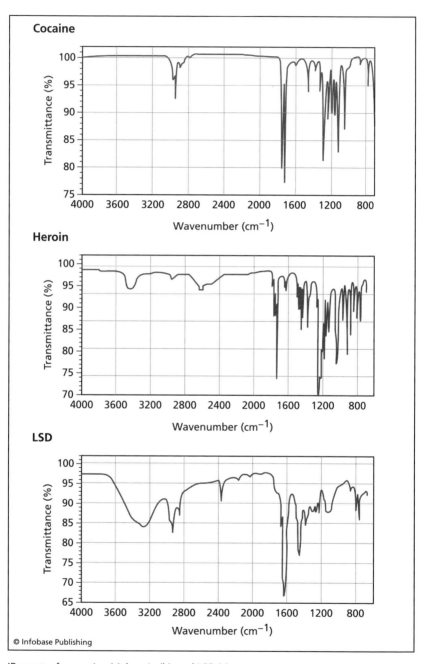

IR spectra for cocaine (a), heroin (b), and LSD (c)

used as confirmatory tests for drugs and poisons that might have been indicated by earlier presumptive tests or screenings. The infrared spectra for three common drugs, cocaine, heroin, and LSD, are shown in the diagram on page 90.

Probably the most popular method now used for confirming the presence of a specific compound in a sample being tested uses a combination of two tests familiar to many high school chemistry students: gas chromatography (GC) and mass spectrometry (MS). The two tests are carried out in tandem to identify compounds present in a sample.

Chromatography is a method for separating a mixture—often a complex mixture—into its component parts. It was invented in the early 1900s by the Russian botanist Mikhail Semenovich Tswett (1872–1919) as a means of separating the various pigments found in plants. Various kinds of chromatography are available, but all

Paper chromatography is the original method by which components of a mixture are separated by passing them across a supporting material to which they adhere differentially. (Andrew Lambert Photography/Photo Researchers, Inc.)

◄ MIKHAIL SEMENOVICH TSWETT (1872–1919) ►

"Think outside the box!" That popular expression is one that encourages people to try to look at problems in new ways, to ignore old answers or old ways of dealing with issues, and to find new approaches for challenging puzzles. "Thinking outside the box" was how the Russian botanist Mikhail Tswett discovered the process of chromatography in the early 1900s.

Mikhail Semenovich Tswett was born in Asti, Italy, on May 14, 1872. His parents had arrived in Italy a few weeks earlier, planning to spend their vacation at Lake Maggiore, near the Swiss border. Tswett's mother died shortly after he was born, and his father took the baby to Lausanne, Switzerland, where he was to spend the next 24 years of his life. Tswett's father returned to Russia but came back to Switzerland every year for extended vacations that he shared with his son.

After completing high school, the younger Tswett enrolled at the University of Geneva, where he majored in botany. For his doctoral thesis, Tswett examined the various pigments (such as chlorophyll, the carotenoids, and the phycobilins) that occur in plants and the methods by which they can be extracted from plants. One of his first discoveries was that various solvents were more or less effective in dissolving these pigments from plant material. For example, some pigments dissolve readily in ethanol or acetone but not in other common organic solvents, such as petroleum ether and ligroin. This "discovery" was not original with Tswett—it was common knowledge among botanical researchers. But those researchers did not give much thought to the phenomenon, attributing it to a matter of some pigments being more soluble in some solvents, and other pigments, in other solvents.

Tswett, however, suggested an alternative explanation. The reason for the differential solubility of pigments in various solvents, he said, was that those compounds were bonded more or less strongly to the plant tissue in which they occurred. Solvents that were able to overcome these bonding

are based on a simple principle: When a mixture of substances is passed over a fixed base, the individual substances in that mixture have varying tendencies to adhere to that base. After the mixture has

forces could dissolve a pigment, while those that could not overcome those forces could not dissolve a pigment.

And thus was born the idea of chromatography. If this explanation describes the way pigments bind naturally with different strengths in plants, then maybe a technique could be developed in which a mixture of pigments could be passed through a column containing a solid phase to which the pigments would bond more or less strongly and, thus, become separated during the process. Tswett announced his discovery of chromatography in a paper entitled "On a New Category of Adsorption Phenomena and Their Application to Biochemical Analysis," presented at a meeting of the Biological Section of the Warsaw Society of Natural Sciences on March 8, 1903.

Shortly after finishing his doctoral studies at Geneva in 1896, Tswett decided to return to Russia and seek a university appointment there. The Russian academic community generally did not accept degrees from other universities, however, so he had to begin his doctoral studies over. In 1901, five years after returning to Russia, he was awarded a Ph.D. in botany from the University of Kazan. He then accepted a position at the University of Warsaw, in a region of Poland then occupied by Russia. He remained at the University of Warsaw until 1908, when he moved to the Polytechnic Institute in the same city.

Tswett was forced to flee Warsaw in 1915 when German troops entered the city. He was unemployed until 1917, when he was able to find a post at the University of Tartu, in present-day Estonia. Within a year, he had to abandon his academic post again, however, when the Germans overran the area in which he was living. At the end of 1918, he found yet another job, this time at the State University of Voronezh, in Russia. By this time, however, he was quite ill, and he died less than a year later, on June 26, 1919.

Tswett's name is sometimes spelled with a *v* (Tsvett) because the letter *w* in German is pronounced as "v." Ironically, the word *tswett* in German means "color," a fitting congruity with the discovery he made. He is widely known today as the father of chromatography.

passed over the base, the components of which it is made are deposited at different positions on the base. The base can then be analyzed to determine what each of the components of the mixture is.

In forensic science, the most common type of chromatography used is gas chromatography. In gas chromatography, the substance to be analyzed is first vaporized, as shown in the diagram below, and mixed with an inert gas, the *mobile phase* in the process. The two gases most commonly used in this process are nitrogen and helium. The carrier gas and the sample to be tested are then passed through a gas column. A thin layer of some material is deposited on the inside of the column walls, providing the *stationary phase* for the process. As the carrier gas and dissolved sample pass through the glass tube, the components of the sample are attracted in varying degrees to the material in the thin layer. Those most attracted to the thin layer will be deposited near the top of the tube, while those less strongly attracted will be carried farther down the column before they are deposited on the inside of the tube. As the carrier gas flows out the bottom of the tube and exits, a sensing device detects the individual components of the mixture. The detector then converts this information to an electrical signal that can be registered by the

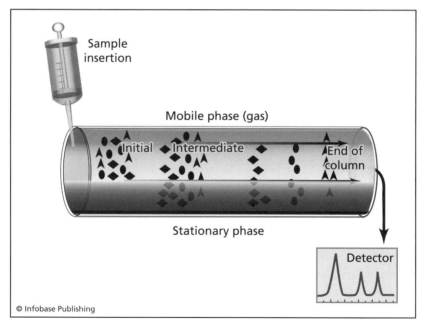

© Infobase Publishing

Gas chromatograph

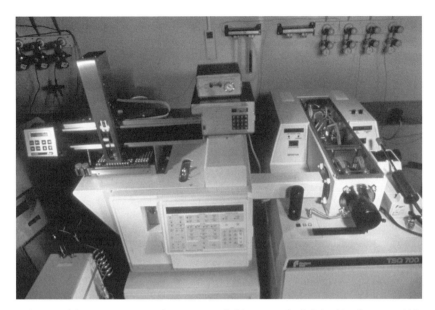

In forensic laboratories, a gas chromatograph (shown at the left in this photograph) is usually connected with a mass spectrometer (shown at the right). (Dr. Jurgen Scriba/ Photo Researchers, Inc.)

recorder as a graph showing the concentration of various substances detected over a period of time.

The recording, known as a *chromatogram,* provides a visual record of the number and type of components present in the original sample. A sample chromatogram is shown on page 96. It shows the number of components present in the original sample, the probable identity of those components, and the relative concentration of each component. The tester identifies the components obtained in any given experiment by comparing the chromatogram with a library of chromatograms for many different substances. Chromatogram libraries, requiring paid registration for viewing, are sometimes available online.

Gas chromatography is a popular analytical tool because it is so sensitive. It is capable of detecting material at nanogram (10^{-9}g) levels. The major problem with chromatograms is that they are not conclusive tests. That is, chromatograms for two or more substances may be so similar that it is impossible to tell which of the substances is present in any given case. When gas chromatography

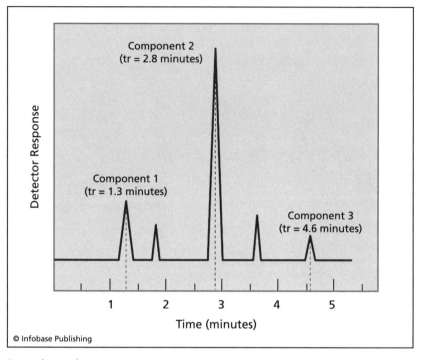

A sample gas chromatogram

is paired with mass spectrometry, however, this disadvantage is overcome.

The second element in the GC/MS system used in forensic analysis is the mass spectrograph, first invented in 1919 by the English physicist Francis William Aston (1877–1945). The basic principle on which the mass spectrometer is based is that the path taken by a charged particle moving through a magnetic field is dependent on the electrical charge (e) and the mass (m) of that particle. The governing equation for this phenomenon is:

$$\frac{e}{m} = \frac{2V}{B^2r^2},$$

where V is the voltage applied to the instrument, B is the strength of the magnetic field, and r is the radius of the path followed by the charged particle.

In a GC/MS system, the individual components produced in the gas chromatograph are transmitted from that device into a mass spectrometer. The figure below shows a schematic diagram of the mass spectrometer. As the components obtained from gas chromatography enter the spectrometer, they are bombarded with electrons, a process that results in the loss of a single electron from each of the molecules present in the mixture. The molecules then become positively charged ions and can be represented by the expression e/m, where e is the same for all molecules, and m is unique for every molecule of the type likely to be encountered in this analysis.

The charged molecules are then accelerated by a voltage through a magnetic field of strength. Each type of molecule will follow a slightly different path depending on its own value of e/m. A detector placed at the back of the spectrometer detects the specific path taken by each type of molecule that enters the instrument. Then, knowing the values of V and B (set for the machine) and observed for r, the tested can determine the value of e/m for each different kind of molecule in the original sample.

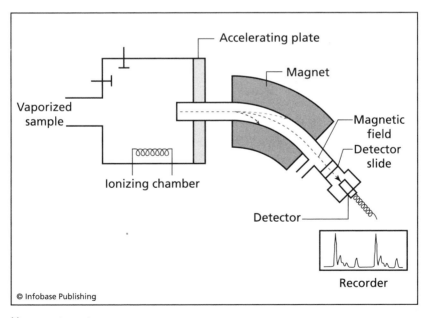

Mass spectrometer

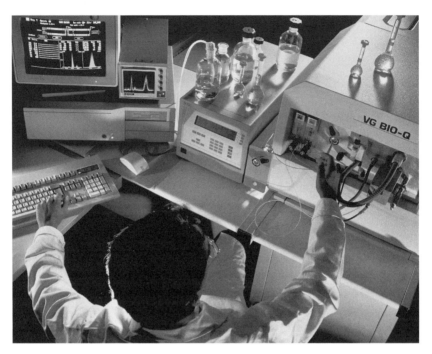

A scientist inserts a sample to be tested into the mass spectrometer shown here. (G. Tompkinson/Photo Researchers, Inc.)

The result of this analysis is a spectrogram of the type shown on page 99. The three spectrograms shown in this figure illustrate the fact that the more complex the molecule, the more complex the spectrogram that will be produced.

The availability of a host of screening and presumptive tests, along with a handful of powerful confirmatory tests, now makes it possible for forensic chemists to analyze many kinds of unknown substances, ranging from pure but complex compounds to highly complex mixtures, with a significant likelihood of obtaining reliable results. Results of chemical tests as well as confirmatory results from gas chromatography and mass spectrometers make it possible to identify a wide range of illegal drugs and poisons. Today it is not unusual for an analyst to obtain nearly proof-positive results on samples of no more than a few micrograms in short periods of time. These identifications often provide strong evidence that make possible the apprehension and conviction of individuals involved in many different kinds of crimes.

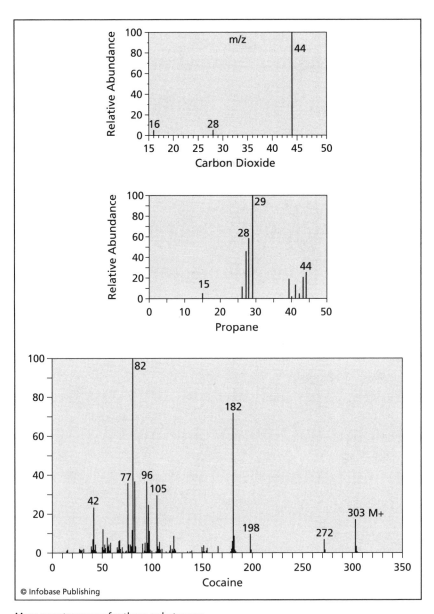

Mass spectrograms for three substances

5

ARSON AND EXPLOSIVES INVESTIGATIONS

A rson and explosives detonation have become problems of considerable interest to the general public in the last decade. News broadcasts carry frequent reports of groups and individuals who set fires or explosives in terrorist attacks around the world. These events represent a changing trend in the use of arson and explosives by criminals and terrorists. At one time, forensic scientists were most concerned about fires set by businesspeople trying to collect on their hazard insurance or by youngsters or adults simply fascinated by fires. Today a far greater range of people are using fires and explosives to make political statements that result in the death and injury of innocent people.

Arson as an Economic and Social Problem

Arson is one of the most common and most serious problems faced by forensic scientists. Arson is defined as the willful or malicious burning of property, usually with criminal or fraudulent intent. For example, a business owner might arrange to have his or her building burned down in order to collect insurance money. Or an individual might burn down someone else's building because of bad feelings between the two people. Or a person might set fire to a structure just for the pleasure of watching it burn. Arsonists of this kind are often called firebugs.

Arson is the second-leading cause of fires in the United States today, exceeded only by smoking. In 2005, according to a report by Michael J. Karter of the National Fire Protection Association, 315 Americans were killed by intentionally set fires. About 31,500 structure fires, 6 percent of all such fires, were set by arsonists. These fires resulted in a total cost of $664 million in property damage, about 6 percent of the total property damage caused by fires. In addition to structural fires, about 21,000 vehicle fires were attributed to arson or other suspicious causes, adding an addition $113 million to the cost of arson fires in the United States. Arson fires cause more than death and property damage—they also displace families who have lost their homes in such fires. In 2000, the American Red Cross reported that they had helped to relocate 76,276 families who had lost their homes due to fires, more than half of all the families assisted by the organization in that year.

Arson Investigations

Arson presents one of the most challenging types of crime forensic chemists encounter. In many cases, a building or vehicle has been badly damaged or totally destroyed by a fire. The fire scene is typically covered with burned wood, charred concrete, partially melted metals, and other materials that provide only fragmentary evidence as to the events that occurred before and during the fire. In addition, such materials are often soaked with water used by firefighters, who may also have cut apart, pulled down, or otherwise damaged materials originally present at the scene.

These factors severely complicate the task of analysis for the forensic chemist and often limit his or her contributions to solving a crime. Sometimes forensic scientists can only identify suspicious materials present at the fire scene. However, this contribution can be an important one, because the presence of certain materials at the scene of a fire can strongly suggest whether the fire was intentionally set. For example, the presence of kerosene or gasoline where such materials would normally not be found or expected suggests that the fire was set intentionally.

As a consequence, the forensic chemist's primary task in the investigation of possible arson fires is to identify accelerants and/or explosives that may have been present at the site of the fire. This information can then be used in combination with other types of evidence collected by law enforcement officials to arrest and convict persons responsible for an arson crime.

Fire is a form of *combustion,* an oxidation reaction in which noticeable heat and light are produced. Such reactions are known, in general, as *exothermic reactions* because heat (*-thermo*) is given off (*exo-*) during the chemical change.

One of the simplest combustion reactions is the one that takes place between carbon and oxygen:

◄ HEAT OF COMBUSTION OF SOME COMMON FUELS ►

SUBSTANCE	HEAT OF COMBUSTION
Wood (pine)	18 kJ/g; 7,500 Btu/lb
Coal, anthracite	31 kJ/g; 13,000 Btu/lb
Coal, bituminous	32 kJ/g; 13,500 Btu/lb
Natural gas	49 kJ/g; 20,000 Btu/lb; 850 Btu/ft^3
Gasoline	48 kJ/g; 20,000 Btu/lb
Diesel oil	47 kJ/g; 19,500 Btu/lb
Charcoal	34 kJ/g; 14,000 Btu/lb
Hydrogen	142 kJ/g; 59,000 Btu/lb; 77 Btu/ft^3

$$C + O_2 \rightarrow CO_2$$

In this case, carbon is oxidized because it has lost electrons to oxygen, which in turn has been reduced. The amount of heat produced in this reaction is known as the heat of combustion. The heat of combustion for the oxidation of pure carbon is about 33 kJ/g (kilojoules per gram), or 14,093 Btu/lb (British thermal units per pound). The heat of combustion for some common fuels are given in the chart on page 102.

The conditions needed for combustion to occur are sometimes represented by means of the *fire triangle,* whose three components are (1) a substance that can be oxidized, the fuel; (2) an oxidizing agent, usually oxygen itself; and (3) sufficient heat to initiate the reaction between the fuel and the oxidizing agent. Although combustion reactions are exothermic overall, they generally require the input of some minimum amount of energy, such as that provided by a match, to initiate the reaction. This energy is needed to break the chemical bonds present in the reactants (the fuel and oxidizing agent), after which sufficient energy is released to maintain the reaction and allow it to proceed exothermically overall.

Because the energy required to break the oxygen-oxygen bonds in an oxygen molecule is constant, the amount of heat needed to initiate any specific combustion reaction depends primarily on the fuel. The amount of energy required for combustion of a substance to begin is its *ignition temperature.* The ignition temperature is defined as the lowest temperature at which a substance will begin to burn and then continue to burn without the additional application of external heat. Ignition temperature is also known as ignition point or kindling point. Ignition temperatures are determined experimentally. The ignition temperatures of some common fuels are shown in the chart on page 104.

Discussions of fires usually refer to the combustion of all kinds of fuels, solids, liquids, and gases. Yet, in fact, the only state in which combustion actually occurs is in the gaseous state. In order for a solid or liquid to catch fire, it must first be converted into one or more combustible gases. For example, when gasoline is heated with a flame, the first change that occurs is vaporization of some portion

◀ **IGNITION TEMPERATURES OF SOME COMMON FUELS** ▶

SUBSTANCE	IGNITION TEMPERATURE
Wood (varies with type)	190–250°C (90–120°F)
Paper	232°C (450°F)
Benzene	562°C (1,044°F)
Carbon monoxide	609°C (1,128°F)
Acetone	538°C (1,000°F)
Gasoline (octane)	220°C (428°F)
Kerosene	254°C (490°F)
Petroleum ether	288°C (550°F)
Turpentine	253°C (488°F)
Hydrogen	585°C (1,085°F)

Source: NAO Gas Composition Data. Available online. URL: http://www.nao.com/ gascompositiontable.htm. (Because various sources give somewhat different values, the above values should be taken as approximations.)

of the gasoline. The vapor can then begin to react with oxygen or some other oxidizing agent rapidly enough for combustion to occur.

The lowest temperature at which a liquid vaporizes sufficiently to permit combustion is known as its *flash point.* If the temperature of the liquid remains lower than its flash point, then no amount of

◄ FLASH POINTS OF SOME TYPICAL FUELS ►

FUEL	FLASH POINT
Ether (diethyl ether)	-49°C (-66°F)
Gasoline	-43°C (-45°F)
Petroleum ether (benzin[e], naphtha, ligroin)	-40°C (-40°F)
Benzene	10°C (50°F)
Ethanol	12.7°C (54.9°F)
Turpentine	34°C (93°F)
Kerosene	80°C (176°F)

Note: Since gasoline, petroleum ether, turpentine, and kerosene are mixtures, their flash points may vary over a considerable range depending on their precise composition. Values given here are typical for the fuel in question.

heat can cause ignition of the fuel. The flash points of some typical liquids are listed in the chart above.

The combustion of a solid is generally a more complex phenomenon than the combustion of a gas or liquid. In some cases, the only necessary step before combustion can occur is that the solid melt and vaporize. Probably the most familiar example of such an instance is the combustion of a candle. When the wick of a candle is lit, the flame provides sufficient heat to melt the wax of which the candle is made. Some portion of the molten wax then vaporizes, providing a gaseous material in which combustion can occur.

In other solids, the changes that take place are more complex and generally involve some chemical change. For example, when wood burns, the molecules that are present first break down to produce gaseous products, such as carbon monoxide and hydrocarbons. These gaseous products then react with oxygen, initiating a combustion reaction. Solids that break down to produce flammable gases when exposed to heat are called pyrolyzable solids. The name comes from the word *pyrolyze,* which means "to decompose or transform a material by subjecting it to heat." Wood and coal are perhaps the most common pyrolyzable solids.

Solids that do not break down to form flammable gases may also undergo combustion, but a different kind of combustion known as *glowing combustion.* Glowing combustion occurs when the molecules on the surface of a solid react with oxygen or some other oxidizing agent rapidly enough to produce noticeable heat and light but not a visible flame. A common example of glowing combustion is seen when the coals remaining after a piece of wood has burned continue to give off heat and light.

One limitation of the fire triangle is that it provides too simplistic a view of the conditions necessary for combustion. The triangle suggests that *any* combination of fuel, oxygen, and heat can result in a fire. That statement is not true, as shown by the preceding discussion of ignition temperature: A minimum temperature is necessary for combustion to occur. Similarly, it is not true that any combination of fuel and oxidizing agent will result in a combustion reaction. Indeed, combustion will *not* take place if the concentration of either fuel or oxidizing agent is too high or too low. Instead, combustion occurs only when the relative amount of these two factors falls within a certain range, known as the *flammable range.*

For example, it is obvious that combustion will not occur in a mixture of 99.9 percent gasoline and 0.1 percent oxygen. In such a mixture, there is simply not enough oxygen available to allow combustion of the gasoline to continue. Conversely, a mixture of 99.9 percent oxygen and 0.1 percent gasoline will also not ignite. In this case, there is too little fuel to permit combustion to continue. In the case of gasoline, the flammable range falls between about 1.5 and 7.6

◁ **FLAMMABLE RANGE OF SOME COMMON FUELS** ▷

FUEL	FLAMMABLE RANGE (PERCENT)
Ether (Ethyl ether)	1.9–36.0
Benzene	1.3–7.1
Ethanol	3.3–19.0
Petroleum ether (benzin, naphtha)	0.8–6.0
Kerosene	0.7–5.0
Gasoline	1.5–7.6
Turpentine	0.8–(no upper limit available)

Source: U.S. Department of Labor, Occupational Safety and Health Administration. "Flammable and Combustible Liquids—1910.106." Available on-line. URL: http://www.osha.gov/SLTC/smallbusiness/sec8.html.

percent. The flammable range of some common fuels is given in the chart above.

Investigation of a fire scene usually takes place in two major parts. In the first stage, an investigator looks for physical evidence that suggests where the fire may have started and whether there is reason to believe that it may have been set intentionally. One of the best clues in this phase of the investigation is the pattern formed when a fire occurs. That pattern usually consists of a V-shaped path, in which the origin of the fire is located at the vertex of the V. This pattern occurs because as a fire burns it tends to spread outward from its point of origin. Once the point of origin has been located, an investigator can examine the area below and around that point for signs that accelerants may have been used to initiate the fire—that is, that arson has been committed.

Other types of physical evidence can be used to suggest the possibility of arson. For example, one might find multiple V-shaped patterns at the site of a fire, suggesting that combustion was initiated at more than one point. Such a pattern tends to be unlikely in the case of a natural fire and suggests that an arsonist may have started the fire at more than one location.

Other physical evidence may suggest that arson was *not* the cause of the fire. For example, investigations of electrical wiring near the origin of the fire might indicate that faulty wires may have ignited the fire. In such a case, arson tends to be less likely. Broken gas lines, electrical appliances that have not been turned off, flammable chemicals, or cigarette butts at the scene of the fire may also indicate that a fire occurred by accident, rather than having been set intentionally.

Arson dogs and mechanical devices are both useful in locating the origin of a fire and, in some cases, providing presumptive evidence for any accelerants present in the area. Dogs are generally trained not only to locate the origin of a fire and the presence of accelerants but also to respond to specific kinds of accelerants. Some dogs are able to identify a dozen or more different kinds of accelerants and respond specifically to those materials at the site of a fire.

A variety of devices are available for on-site investigation of accelerant residues. These include

➤ Chemical color test methods, in which dyes are added to materials collected in an area. The dyes produce distinctive color changes with various types of accelerants. One test that is sometimes used is called the *Griess test*. The Griess reagent contains a mixture of sulfanilamide and N-1-naphthylethylenediamine dihydrochloride (NED) acidified with phosphoric acid. This reagent reacts with nitrate ion contained in a residue to produce a characteristic purplish color.

➤ Catalytic combustion detectors that contain a wire coil coated with platinum. When the wire is heated at the scene of the fire, any accelerants remaining in the air will be oxidized, producing a characteristic heat of combustion. The heat of combustion produced can be converted to an electrical signal that can give an immediate readout.

➤ Flame ionization detectors, in which the sample is mixed with hydrogen gas and then ignited. The ionization this method produces in the sample changes the conductivity of the carrier gas inside the device, producing an electrical signal that can be related to that of known accelerants.

➤ Ultraviolet fluoroscopes, which, as their name suggests, illuminate a crime scene with ultraviolet light ("black" light) in which different accelerants glow with different and characteristic light patterns.

➤ Infrared spectrometers, which are portable versions of a common type of laboratory device that analyzes the light given off when a sample is burned within it.

As with many forensic tests, all of the tests listed above are presumptive tests only. They are used to refine inspection of the fire scene. Samples taken from the scene are then subjected to confirmatory tests conducted at a forensics laboratory.

Once the origin of a fire has been located, the investigator's next task is to look for any foreign material—any accelerant—that might have been used in starting the fire. That task might at first appear to be impossible because one might reasonably assume that any flammable chemical used in starting a fire would itself be consumed in the blaze that followed. In fact, such is generally not the case. Small amounts of an accelerant tend to be absorbed by materials present at the scene, such as carpet, wood flooring, and plastic floor tiles. Such materials are generally known as substrates. An arson investigator's task is to remove samples of such materials with sufficient care so that any accelerant residues are not disturbed. Those residues can then be tested with greater specificity at the forensics laboratory.

Samples of the accelerants themselves may sometimes be found at the scene of a fire. "Empty" containers in which the accelerant was carried to the crime scene are usually not entirely empty. The presence of even a few drops of an accelerant is sufficient to permit analytical tests identifying the material used in the crime.

Once potential accelerant samples have been found, they must be treated in such a way as to extract any accelerants present and to prepare them for confirmatory tests. Five major methods are used for the extraction process: steam distillation, vacuum distillation, solvent extraction, charcoal sampling, and headspace sampling.

Steam distillation is one of the oldest and simplest methods of accelerant extraction. The sample removed from the fire scene is added to water in a distilling flask, and the mixture is heated to the boiling point. Any volatile material in the sample that will form an azeotropic mixture with water will boil over in the vapor produced during boiling. (An azeotropic mixture is a liquid mixture of two or more substances that retains the same composition in the vapor state as in the liquid state.) It can then be condensed and captured in the usual method of distillation. The most important limitation on this procedure, of course, is that any accelerant present in the fire sample must form an azeotropic mixture with water. The method cannot be used, then, for liquids such as ethanol and acetone.

Vacuum distillation is similar to steam distillation, except it takes place under reduced pressure. Under those conditions, the boiling point of the water-sample mixture is reduced, and possible damage to the fire sample is also reduced. Vacuum distillation is used when the higher temperatures needed for steam distillation are likely to damage the sample; for example, when the sample consists of charred pieces of paper.

Solvent extraction, as the name suggests, makes use of some solvent in which accelerants thought to be present in a sample are soluble. The solvent (usually n-pentane, n-hexane, carbon disulfide, or methylene chloride) is added to the sample, and sufficient time is allowed for the dissolving of any soluble accelerant present. The solvent is then allowed to evaporate to see if the desired accelerant(s) are left behind for analysis. One situation in which solvent extraction might be used is that in which the substrate is a nonporous material, such as glass or metal.

Charcoal sampling is a simple and powerful tool for extracting accelerants from a sample. In the process, a strip of activated charcoal (finely divided charcoal) or a wire coated with charcoal is suspended in the air above the sample to be analyzed in a closed container. Over a period of time, accelerants in the sample are adsorbed to the surface of the carbon. The container may be warmed to increase the rate at which *adsorption* occurs. After about an hour, the charcoal strip or wire is removed and immersed in a solvent, such as n-hexane or carbon disulfide. The accelerants dissolve in the solvent and are then recovered by permitting the solvent to evaporate.

Headspace sampling is perhaps the most common method of accelerant extraction used in forensic laboratories. In one form of the technique, the sample is placed in a closed container with two holes, as shown in the diagram below. Some carrier gas, such as argon, nitrogen, or room air, passes into the container through one hole. Vapors from any accelerants present in the sample mix with

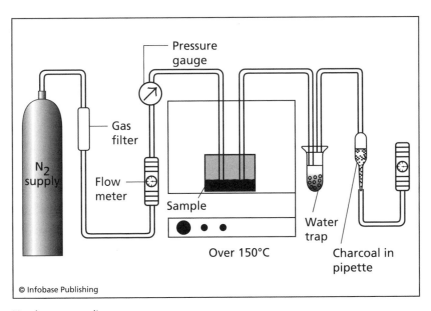

© Infobase Publishing

Headspace sampling

the carrier gas and are removed through the second hole. The container may be warmed to increase the rate at which accelerants evaporate and are removed from the container. After the carrier-accelerant mixture leaves the container, it is passed through a charcoal filter, where accelerants are adsorbed and removed from the carrier gas.

In one variation of this procedure, a syringe is inserted into a single hole in the top of the container, and a sample of vapors present in the space above the sample (the headspace) is removed. The sample can then be injected directly into a gas chromatograph, where its composition is analyzed. The most serious drawback with this variation is that the size of the syringe used for extraction limits the size of the sample that can be extracted and analyzed.

Headspace extraction is popular because it is among the most sensitive of all extraction techniques and can be used with virtually any substrate. It does, however, require more sophisticated equipment than most other extraction methods, and it can be used only once on a given sample.

The most popular method for analyzing the composition of substances extracted from a sample by the various procedures just described is gas chromatography. This testing method was described in chapter 4. The value of gas chromatography lies in its ability to differentiate among the many hydrocarbons that are present in gasoline, kerosene, and other commonly used accelerants. Although the specific chromatogram for any given petroleum product is unique, various gasoline samples, kerosene samples, turpentine samples, and the like are sufficiently similar to allow a relatively positive identification of accelerants present in a sample.

The diagram on page 113 shows chromatograms obtained for samples of gasoline and turpentine. A chromatogram for gasoline obtained from a different refinery at a different time will vary to some degree from that shown in the graph. However, it will bear no resemblance at all to the chromatogram for turpentine. The distinctive character of chromatograms makes it possible to use them as confirmatory tests for nearly all common accelerants.

The use of chromatography has revolutionized the science of arson investigation. The procedure makes possible the identification of trace amounts of accelerants that confirm whether a fire has been set intentionally or has occurred accidentally.

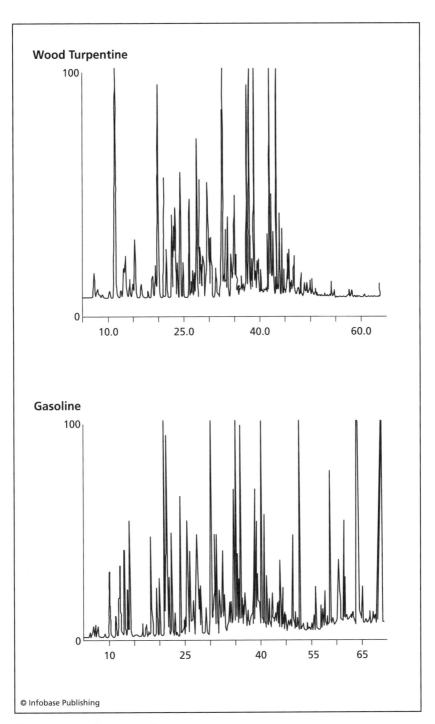

Chromatograms for two accelerants

◁ PAUL LELAND KIRK (1902–1970) ▷

"The standard in its field." That description is an honor with special significance to any professional. It is an acknowledgment that one has attained the highest possible achievement in some academic discipline. And that is the recognition that is usually given to the book *Fire Investigation* by Paul Leland Kirk, first published in 1969 and now in its fifth edition. The book provides a comprehensive treatment of virtually every aspect of fire investigation theory and practice, including all types of fires, arson, and explosions; fundamental chemical and physical aspects of fires; on-site investigations; and laboratory analysis of accelerants, explosives, and other fire-related evidence.

Paul Leland Kirk was born in Colorado Springs, Colorado, on May 9, 1902. After attending local schools, he enrolled at the Randolph-Macon Academy in Fort Royal, Virginia. He then transferred to Ohio State University, from which he graduated in 1924. Kirk then moved to the University of Pittsburgh, where he was awarded his master's degree in chemistry in 1925. He completed his formal education at the University of California in Berkeley, from which he received his Ph.D. in biochemistry in 1927. As is often the case with doctoral students, Kirk was employed as a teaching assistant at the university while working on his degree. After graduation, he was appointed research fellow in biochemistry. Over the next decade, he was promoted to assistant professor, associate professor, and, finally, full professor of biochemistry in 1945. During World War II, he was on leave of absence from the university while working on the Manhattan Project, through which the first atomic bomb was developed and built.

During the early 1940s, Kirk became interested in the application of scientific information and techniques to the solution of forensic problems. After the war, he not only returned to his post at the university but also opened his own consulting firm in the field of forensic analysis. He soon became widely recognized as an authority in the field and, along with criminal expert and Berkeley police chief August Vollmer, was asked to establish the School of Criminology at the University of California at Berkeley.

Some authorities argue that Kirk's greatest contribution to forensic science was in defining the approach that one should follow in analyzing a crime. Until the 1950s, most forensic scientists were specialists in other fields (biology, chemistry, physics, and so on) who applied their specialized knowledge to some aspect of forensic analysis. Kirk argued that criminology was and ought to be a specialized field in and of itself in which the forensic scientist was able to draw on information and practices from a wide variety of scientific and nonscientific disciplines.

In addition, Kirk strongly emphasized a principle sometimes known as *individualization,* the concept that any individual piece of evidence of whatever kind can be conclusively linked to the presence of a specific individual at the crime scene. The problem for the forensic scientist is to find that evidence and make the irrevocable connection between it and the perpetrator of the crime.

During his life, Kirk became a popular expert witness in a number of criminal cases. Perhaps the most famous of those cases involved the trial of Dr. Samuel H. Sheppard, accused of killing his wife in 1954. Kirk provided evidence that Mrs. Sheppard's killer was left-handed. Although Dr. Sheppard was right-handed, he was convicted of the crime. That conviction was overturned 12 years later, to a large degree because of Kirk's testimony.

Paul Kirk is a major figure in the history of forensic science, not only for his classic textbook on fire investigations, but also for his efforts to make criminology a profession. In 1963, he wrote a now-famous article for the *Journal of Criminal Law, Criminology, and Police Science* in which he asked "Is Criminalistics a Profession?" Kirk confessed that he did not know the answer to the question but suggested the criteria that had to be met if forensic scientists were to think of themselves as "professionals." They would have to develop a formal program of education, design and adopt a code of ethics, and find ways to demonstrate competence in their field if they were to be recognized by others as professionals.

Kirk made important contributions to the accomplishment of those goals. For example, he helped establish the first school of criminology in the United States. Working with Vollmer, Kirk helped establish the Institute of Criminology and Criminalists at the University of California in 1937. Thirteen years later, Kirk and Vollmer collaborated again to oversee the establishment of the nation's first formal school of criminology in a major university, located at the University of California. He remained affiliated with that program until his death in Berkeley on June 5, 1970.

In addition to *Fire Investigation,* Kirk wrote a number of other books on forensic science, including *Density and Refractive Index: Their Applications in Criminal Identification* (1951), *Crime Investigation: Physical Evidence and Police Laboratory Interscience* (1953), and *The Crime Laboratory* (1965; with Lowell W. Bradford). Kirk continued in his post at the School of Criminology until his retirement in 1967.

Explosives Investigations

Explosives are compounds or mixtures that undergo rapid chemical or nuclear reactions that result in the formation of large volumes of gas, usually at high temperatures. The gases formed in the reaction expand outward rapidly, producing a shock wave. The shock wave is usually responsible for most of the immediate damage caused by the explosion, such as the splitting of rock or the destruction of buildings. A secondary effect of an explosion is the fire that results when flammable materials are ignited by the heat of the explosion. The composition of explosive devices can be modified to alter the relative amount of shock and fire damage.

Until the 19th century, the only type of explosive known was the chemical explosive referred to as gunpowder or black powder. The first mention of such a material was in a Chinese book, *Classified Essentials of the Mysterious Tao of the True Origin of Things*, written in about 850 C.E. Gunpowder is a mixture of charcoal, sulfur, and potassium nitrate (nitre). When gunpowder is ignited, its compounds react with each other to form a variety of gases, including carbon monoxide, carbon dioxide, sulfur dioxide, and nitric oxide. No single chemical equation adequately represents the variety of reactions that occur among the three reactants during the explosion. The heat released during the reaction causes the gases to expand rapidly, forming shock waves.

Explosives are classified based on a variety of characteristics, such as their chemical composition, rate of reaction, or use. The most common system for classifying explosives divides them into low explosives and high explosives and further splits each of these large classes into more specific subcategories.

Low explosives are compounds or mixtures that burn rather than explode. The damage they cause results more from the heat and flames they produce than from any shock wave that may occur. Low explosives usually begin burning at one surface, after which a flame moves slowly through the mass of the material. The two most common low explosives are gunpowder and smokeless powder. The latter is generally available in two forms: single-base powder, which contains either nitrocellulose or nitrated cotton, and double-base powder, which contains a mixture of nitroglycerin and nitrocellulose.

Low explosives are used as propellants for bullets, fireworks, and rockets and in safety fuses. Safety fuses are made by wrapping gunpowder in a casing made of plastic or fabric. When ignited at one end, the gunpowder burns slowly along the length of the wire until it reaches another type of explosive (a high explosive) that is ignited by the flame. Although low explosives are characterized by their tendency to burn rather than to explode, they may react more violently if they are confined. In such a case, the heat and gases produced during combustion are unable to escape into the surrounding air and may build to a point where the mixture explodes.

Although gunpowder and smokeless powder are the most common types of low explosives, many other variations are possible. In general, all that is required is a strong oxidizing agent (such as potassium nitrate) and one or more reducing agents (such as charcoal or sulfur). Other common oxidizing agents include potassium perchlorate ($KClO_4$), potassium chlorate ($KClO_3$), ammonium perchlorate (NH_4ClO_4), barium nitrate ($Ba(NO_3)_2$), and sodium peroxide (Na_2O_2). Other possible reducing agents include phosphorus, magnesium filings, starch, and sawdust.

High explosives are compounds or mixtures that quickly detonate throughout every part of their mass. The chemical reactions that cause the explosion are often completed within a few microseconds after ignition. One measure of the effectiveness of an explosive is its *rate of detonation,* the speed at which an expanding gas moves outward from the point of detonation. The chart on page 118 lists the rates of detonation of some common explosives.

High explosives are subdivided into two classes, *primary explosives* and *secondary explosives.* Primary explosives are sensitive and unstable and may be detonated easily by the application of heat, mechanical shock, or an electric spark. Some typical primary explosives are lead azide ($Pb(N_3)_2$), mercury fulminate (mercury cyanate; $Hg(CNO)_2$), lead styphnate (lead trinitroresorcinate; $[C_6H(NO_2)_3(PbO_2)]$), diazodinitrophenol [$(NO_2)_2C_6H_2ON_2$], and tetracene (tetrazene; $H_2NC(:NH)NHNHN:NC(:NH)NHNHNO$). Because these compounds are so unstable, they are often used to ignite other

◁ RATE OF DETONATION OF SOME COMMON EXPLOSIVES ▷

EXPLOSIVE	RATE OF DETONATION*
Gunpowder	400 m/s; 1,300 ft/s
Lead azide	4,600 m/s; 15,000 ft/s
Mercury fulminate	5,000 m/s; 16,000 ft/s
Ammonium nitrate	1,750 m/s; 5,700 ft/s
C-4	8,000 m/s; 26,500 ft/s
HMX	9,000 m/s; 30,000 ft/s
Nitroglycerin	4,600 m/s; 15,000 ft/s
PETN	8,250 m/s; 27,000 ft/s
RDX	8,200 m/s; 26,800 ft/s
TNT	7,000 m/s; 22,000 ft/s

*Values given are averages

explosives, such as in the form of a blasting cap. A blasting cap is a small container filled with an explosive that is used to detonate other explosives. The blasting cap is usually detonated by means of an electrical current. Because they are so difficult and dangerous to work with, primary explosives are rarely used by amateurs in the construction of homemade bombs.

Secondary explosives are more stable than primary explosives. If ignited in open air, they tend to burn quietly rather than exploding.

However, when detonated by another explosive, such as a blasting cap, they explode in much the same way as primary explosives. Some common secondary explosives are dynamite (a generic term for a wide variety of explosives whose primary component is nitroglycerin or ammonium nitrate); TNT (trinitrotoluene; $CH_3C_6H_2(NO_2)_3$); RDX (cyclotrimethylenetrinitramine; cyclonite; $N(NO_2)CH_2N(NO_2)CH_2N(NO_2)CH_2$); and PETN (pentaerythritol tetranitrate; $C(CH_2ONO_2)_4$). At least two dozen other secondary explosives are used and generally available, many of them combinations or variations of the four basic explosives listed. For example, Octol is a mixture consisting of 75 percent HMX and 25 percent TNT; Torpex is a mixture of 37–41 percent TNT, 41–45 percent RDX, and 18 percent powdered aluminum; and Minol-2 contains 40 percent TNT, 40 percent ammonium nitrate, and 20 percent powdered aluminum.

For nearly a century after its discovery by the Swedish chemist Alfred Nobel (1833–96), dynamite was the most popular secondary explosive for use in industry and the military. In recent years, however, dynamite has been replaced in most applications by safer, less expensive alternatives based on compounds of ammonia. These explosives are usually prepared in one of three formulations: water gels, emulsions, and ANFO explosives. Water gel explosives were first made available commercially in 1958. They consisted of a mixture of ammonium nitrate, TNT, water, a gelatinizing agent (usually guar gum), and a bonding agent (such as borax). Later, gels were made more powerful and efficient by the addition of aluminum and other metallic components and by the development of better gelatinizing agents. Water gels are popular in industry because they are water-resistant, very powerful per gram of weight, safe, and flexible enough to be shaped into almost any desired form.

As their name suggests, emulsions consist of two phases, one oil and one water. The water phase is a supersaturated solution of ammonium nitrate, while the oil phase is a hydrocarbon fuel, such as diesel oil or fuel oil. An emulsion between the two liquids is made possible by the use of an emulsifying agent, such as sodium dodecylsulfate or sorbitan monooleate. Emulsions are popular as industrial explosives for most of the same reasons as water gels. For example, they can be transported to a construction site in a larger tanker truck and sprayed directly into the region where they are to be used. They provide a powerful explosive in an expensive, easily transportable form.

ANFO explosives get their name from their two primary components, *ammonium nitrate* and *fuel oil*. One of their most attractive properties is ease of preparation. They can be made by simply soaking ammonium nitrate in the fuel oil. The moist mixture can then be packaged and safely transported, ready for detonation at an industrial location. In fact, their ease of preparation has made ANFO explosives popular among terrorists and other criminals. Perhaps the best-known example of the use of ANFO explosives by a terrorist was the 1995 bombing of the Alfred P. Murrah Federal Building in Oklahoma City by Timothy McVeigh. McVeigh made his explosive device by soaking readily available commercial fertilizer in ordinary fuel oil. The device was powerful enough to blow apart the Murrah building, killing 168 people.

The popularity of ammonium-based explosives in the United States is reflected in the fact that they now account for about 99 percent of all explosives used in industry, as reported in the U.S. Geological Survey's *Minerals Yearbook* 2005. More than two-thirds of those explosives are used by the coal mining industry, with quarrying and nonmetal mining, metal mining, and construction work making up the remaining one-third of explosions used in the nation.

Improvements in explosion technology over the past few decades have been a boon to industry, which now has a variety of relatively safe, inexpensive, powerful explosives to use in mining, construction, and other applications. The ease with which these explosives can be made, transported, and used, however, has also made them an attractive material for individual terrorists like Timothy McVeigh and members of al-Qaeda, the Arab Islamist terrorist group that bombed the World Trade Center in New York in 1993.

As with fire accelerants, forensic scientists have now developed a number of techniques for locating, collecting, and identifying explosives that may have been used in the commission of a crime. These techniques fall into two general categories. First are those methods used for analyzing the residues left at the site of a bombing in order to determine the type of explosive(s) used in that act. Second are those methods used for screening individuals and cargo that have the potential for use in terrorist or other kinds of criminal activity.

As is the case with arson investigations, the goal of a forensic scientist in examining the site of an explosion is to locate the point at which the explosive was detonated, collect samples of the explosive that may have been left at the site, and carry out tests that may determine the nature of the explosive. The first step is usually straightforward since an explosion almost always leaves a crater at the point of detonation. Almost invariably, some residue of the unexploded material will remain embedded in the soil or surrounding materials. An investigator must, therefore, examine these materials carefully for even microscopic particles of the original explosive. In most cases, soil is passed through a fine screen to separate out and collect such particles.

A common and long-used on-site method for determining the identity of an explosion is a color test, similar to the color tests used in arson investigations. The three most common reagents used for such tests are the Griess reagent, diphenylamine, and alcoholic potassium hydroxide (KOH). The Griess reagent was discussed earlier in this chapter. The diphenylamine reagent is made by dissolving one gram (g) of the compound in 100 milliliters (mL) of concentrated sulfuric acid. And the alcoholic KOH reagent is made by dissolving 10 g of potassium hydroxide in 100 mL of absolute ethanol. The chart on page 122 summarizes the colors produced by a variety of common explosives with these three major tests.

As the chart suggests, color tests do not provide much detail as to the specific explosive used in a particular incident. For example, a substance that gives a pink-to-red color with the Griess test, a blue color with the diphenylamine test, and no color with the alcoholic KOH test could be a number of different explosives, including a nitrate, nitroglycerin, PETN, or RDX. Color tests are therefore useful primarily as screening tests for substances that must undergo more sophisticated techniques in the forensic laboratory.

At one time, most of these technologies required fairly sophisticated equipment, often of considerable size—a factor that limited their uses to the forensic laboratory itself. Advances in technology

◄ COLOR TESTS FOR SOME COMMON EXPLOSIVES ►

SUBSTANCE	GRIESS TEST	DIPHENYL-AMINE TEST	ALCOHOLIC KOH TEST
Chlorates	None	Blue	None
Nitrates	Pink to red	Blue	None
Nitrocellulose	Pink	Dark blue	None
nitroglycerin	Pink to red	Blue	None
PETN	Pink to red	Blue	None
RDX	Pink to red	Blue	None
TNT	None	None	Red
Tetryl	Pink to red	Blue	Reddish-violet

have made it possible to design smaller equipment. Equipment sizes for some tests have reduced to a degree that they can be used for on-site testing of explosives. The same technologies can also be used at airports, seaports, and other locations to screen luggage, cargo, and individuals.

An example of the kind of portable explosive detection and identification system that is now widely used by forensic investigators is the EGIS system, manufactured by Thermo Electron of Waltham, Massachusetts. The EGIS system consists of two parts, a gas chromatograph and a chemiluminescent detector. The gas chromatograph works in exactly the same way as the laboratory model described earlier in this chapter. A sample taken from the crime scene is heated and passed through the chromatograph, which separates the explosive mixture into its component parts. The components are then passed into the chemiluminescent detector for final identification.

The chemiluminescent detector operates on the principle that nitrate groups found in most explosive compounds, under the proper circumstances, emit infrared light of characteristic wavelength that can be detected and measured. In the EGIS detector, molecules containing the nitrate group (NO_2^-) are first pyrolyzed to produce nitric oxide (NO). The nitric oxide is then reacted with ozone (O_3) to produce nitric oxide molecules in an excited state (NO_2^*). The excited NO_2^* molecules then decay to a more stable state (NO_2) by emitting a photon of characteristic wavelength that can be detected and identified. The sequence of reactions is as follows:

$$\text{molecules of explosive} \xrightarrow{\text{heat}} NO$$

$$NO + O_3 \rightarrow NO_2^*$$
$$NO_2^* \rightarrow NO_2 + h\nu$$

A second device that has been widely used in the detection and identification of explosive materials is the ion mobility spectrometer (IMS), shown in the diagram on page 124. Air in the vicinity of the explosion site is drawn into the IMS through the entry port at the left in the diagram. Just inside this port is a radioactive material, usually nickel-63. Radiation emitted by the radioactive material ionizes molecules of any explosion material present, forming positively charged ions. These ions are accelerated by a negative charge at the opposite end of the ionization region, through a gate in the middle of the device, and into the drift region. The rate at which ions travel through the drift region is a function of their mass and charge. That rate has been measured and is well known for the ions of all common explosive materials. As ions drift through the device, they eventually come into contact with a detector plate at the end of the

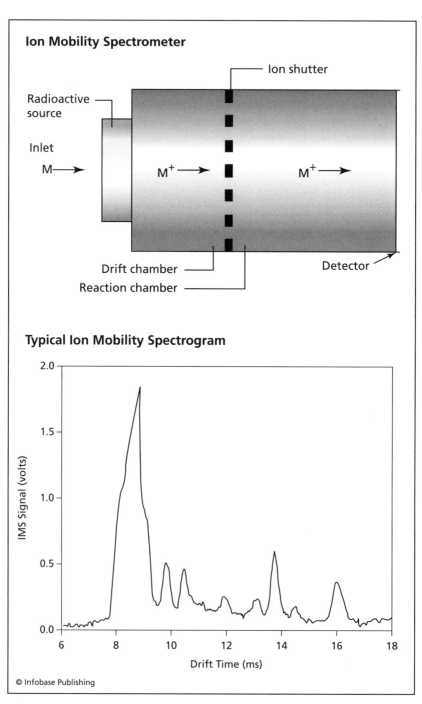

Ion mobility spectrometer and typical spectrogram

IMS, where their presence is detected and recorded as an IMS spectrum, similar to the one shown in the accompanying figure. The peaks shown at about 13 and 14 minutes are characteristic of those observed for TNT and two forms of RDX.

A somewhat similar method for detecting the presence of explosives is the electron capture detector (ECD) shown in the diagram on page 126. Air is drawn into the instrument at one portal and mixed with an inert carrier gas, such as argon or helium. The gas mixture passes into the central portion of the device, where a radioactive source causes ionization of the carrier gas and explosive molecules. Electrons released during the ionization process travel to an anode that runs through the center of the chamber. The flow of electrons along this anode into an exterior circuit is measured by an ammeter. In the absence of any explosive molecules, the electrical current will be constant and known for any given voltage applied to the anode. As explosive molecules enter the chamber and are ionized, however, they exert an attraction for some of the electrons being released from the carrier gas. The presence of these explosive molecules, therefore, reduces the number of electrons reaching the anode and, hence, the current observed. Further, the reduction in current will differ for various explosive molecules because of differences in their size and charge. An ECD by itself is not able to identify specific explosive molecules, so it is generally paired with a gas chromatograph to sort out the explosive molecules before they enter the ECD.

Some detection devices use chemical mechanisms that are proprietary information, that is, information that is kept secret by companies that manufacture the devices. One such instrument is the thermo-redox detector (TRD), which is produced by a number of companies, including IDS of Ottawa, Canada. In a TRD instrument, air is drawn into a portal and passed over a coil heated with a proprietary material that is designed to attract molecules of explosives. Once attracted, those molecules are pyrolyzed, and during pyrolyzation, they release nitrogen dioxide gas. The nitrogen dioxide gas is then reduced by a proprietary reaction, and the rate of reduction is recorded by a detection device. IDS's model EVD-3000 weighs less than seven pounds, is ready to operate in about a minute, and gives results in about 15 seconds. It is able to detect most common explosives, including dynamite, nitroglycerin, TNT, C-4, RDX, and PETN, and it costs in the range of about $20,000 per unit.

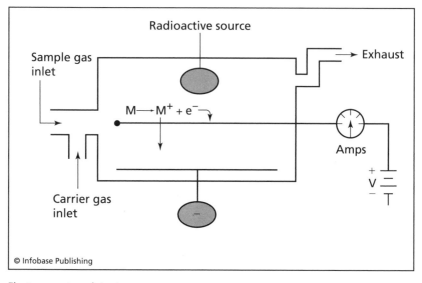

Electron capture detector

An intriguing suggestion for the tracing of explosives was offered in 1973 by Richard G. Livesay, a chemist working at the 3M Corporation in St. Paul, Minnesota. Livesay invented a tiny particle called a *taggant* that could be used to provide a distinctive "fingerprint" for every explosive material manufactured. The particle consists of several layers of a melamine polymer tightly bonded to each other. Most taggants consist of about eight such layers. Each melamine layer has a distinctive color that can be translated numerically using a color-coding system used for electrical resistors. In that system, the color black represents the number 0, brown stands for 1, red for 2, and so on. Taggants are about the size of fine sand or ground pepper, with a minimum dimension of 44 micrometers. When an explosive containing taggants is detonated, most of the taggant particles will be destroyed. The number originally present in the taggant is so great, however, that at least some are certain to survive. The surviving particles can be found by using a magnetic source or ultraviolet light; afterward they can be examined and identified with a pocket microscope of at least 100X magnification.

Taggants are currently not being used in the United States, although they have been required by law in Switzerland since 1980.

The Swiss government reports that taggants have been very helpful in identifying explosives used in the commission of crimes. As of late 2006, however, the United States had not yet decided to require the use of taggant technology in the manufacture of explosives.

Some of the detection devices developed for on-site investigations can be adapted for use as screening tools at sensitive locations through which terrorists or other criminals might be expected to pass. Airports are perhaps the most obvious of these locations. For example, the EGIS detection system described above is now widely used in the United States and other countries to screen luggage checked by passengers on airline flights. The operator of the system wipes a swab across the surface of a passenger's luggage and then places it in a holder attached to the inlet port in the EGIS machine. The swab will pick up even minute particles of explosive material that have come into contact with any part of the luggage, and the EGIS device will detect and send an "alarm" message to the operator. If no such particles are detected, the device registers a "clear" signal. An EGIS test is highly reliable and very fast, usually completed in no more than about 15 seconds. An EGIS detector can be used to scan virtually any kind of surface with which an explosive may have come into contact, including a person's clothing, a vehicle, or a building surface.

Portable, on-site detection devices such as those described here provide preliminary information only, information that can suggest additional lines of research by forensic investigators. In order to obtain definitive identifications of suspected explosives, on-site personnel must send samples to the forensic laboratory, where they are submitted to a GC/MS examination.

Other devices are used to screen larger containers, such as cargo containers. These devices usually incorporate the same technology as that used in computed tomography imaging, otherwise known as CT or CAT scans. In this technology, an object being screened is passed through a tunnel that contains a rotating X-ray source. The X-ray source makes images of the object and its interior composition from a number of different angles. Those images are then assembled into an overall image by a computer and compared to a standard library of similar images for explosive materials. If the machine detects a match between an object being scanned and the

◀ RICHARD G. LIVESAY (1921–) ▶

Among the most difficult kind of crimes to solve today are those that involve the use of explosives. When an explosive is detonated, it is almost entirely destroyed, along with much of the material surrounding the detonation site. It is not difficult to imagine the challenge facing a forensic investigator who must sort through the rubble of a building destroyed by the use of a high-power explosive. During the 1970s, Richard G. Livesay, an employee of the 3M Corporation in St. Paul, Minnesota, devised a method for making the forensic investigator's task somewhat easier: the use of taggants.

Richard G. Livesay was born in Milwaukee, Wisconsin, on August 8, 1921. In correspondence with author David E. Newton, he reports that he first became interested in chemistry as a small boy when he received a chemistry set and began to work his way through the experiments provided with it. Livesay earned his B.S. degree in organic chemistry in 1947 and his M.S. degree in biochemistry in 1958, both from the University of Wisconsin at Madison (UW-Madison). He then completed all of the course work necessary for his Ph.D., but did not present his dissertation.

While still a student at Madison, Livesay worked as a photographic technician at the University of Wisconsin Naval Research Laboratory (1946–49). From 1949 to 1951, he served as head of the chemistry department at Wisconsin State Teacher's College at Whitewater (now the University of Wisconsin at Whitewater), and from 1951 to 1956, he worked as an intelligence officer for the U.S. government. While studying for his master's degree and his Ph.D., he worked as a research assistant in the biochemistry department at UW-Madison.

After leaving UW-Madison in 1959, Livesay took a job as a research specialist and patent liaison at 3M. It was there that he invented the taggant,

standard library of images, it emits a warning signal, indicating that the object should be examined more closely by an operator. The most widely used instrument of this type is the CTX 5500 DS, produced by InVision Technologies of Newark, California.

Few areas of forensic science are developing and changing as rapidly as the detection of explosive materials. The rapid rise of tera microparticle made of thin pieces of melamine plastic of different colors. Taggants inserted into an explosive at the site of manufacture would help investigators determine the company that produced the explosive and, hence, provide a possible clue as to the person who bought it. In later developments, fluorescing dyes were added to taggants to make them more visible to investigators at the scene of a crime.

In 1985, Livesay left 3M to form his new corporation, Microtrace, Inc., to make and sell the taggants he had invented. He served as president and director of technology at Microtrace from 1985 to 1996. Since leaving Microtrace, Livesay has continued to remain active in research, serving as a technical consultant in identification systems. He currently resides with his wife, Corinne, in St. Paul.

Despite their obvious value, taggants have not been widely used in the United States. Some opponents suggest that the addition of taggants to an explosive might contribute to the deterioration of the material. They also worry that the addition of a foreign material—the taggant—might disrupt the delicate balance of chemicals present in an explosive and, perhaps, cause a premature explosion. An unexpressed but likely concern is that explosives manufacturers do not want to be held legally accountable for accidents involving their products.

Those who support the addition of taggants to explosives point to their successful use in Switzerland since 1984. The Swiss government has reported that taggants were used in solving 559 bombing cases in the small country between 1984 and 1996. Proponents point out how helpful taggants could have been in solving the larger number of crimes in which explosives were used in the United States during the same time period. As of the early 2000s, however, the U.S. government has still not authorized the use of these markers in explosives manufactured in the United States. Livesay's exciting discovery has yet to realize its promise in this country.

rorist activities around the world in the early 21st century has made the quick, accurate analysis of transported materials a high priority. The U.S. government has initiated a program to encourage the development and use of smaller devices that are still able to produce fast and accurate screening results. Part of the problem, however, is that research on explosives is going forward at a rapid rate, producing new materials that are effective and efficient for a variety of industrial operations but, at the same time, easy for terrorists and other criminals to make and use. The competition between ever-improving explosives and better-designed detection systems is likely to continue well into the future.

The analysis of crime scenes at which fires and explosions have occurred is a major part of the forensic chemist's job. Today investigators have a wide range of analytical tests and sophisticated equipment with which to study microscopic pieces of evidence collected at such crime scenes. As disgruntled individuals and terrorists continue to use fire and explosives to disrupt society, forensic chemists will go on developing methods for identifying the persons responsible for such events.

6

DNA FINGERPRINTING

In July 1984, Kirk Bloodsworth felt his life was coming unraveled. He had left his home in Cambridge, Massachusetts, to seek reconciliation with his wife in eastern Maryland. When his efforts failed, he disappeared for a week before returning to Cambridge. There he agonized to a friend about the "terrible thing" he had done by abandoning his wife, leaving her with the family's debts.

But Kirk never realized just how difficult his life was to become. On August 7, 1984, he was arrested for the rape and murder of nine-year-old Dawn Hamilton. He had been identified by two teenage boys fishing near the scene of the crime. And Kirk's "terrible thing" comment was reported to police by a Cambridge friend. Kirk's guilt seemed certain, and he was convicted and sentenced to death by a Baltimore County judge in 1985. Kirk successfully appealed his conviction and was retried in 1986. He was again found guilty and, this time, sentenced to two life sentences, without possibility of parole.

In retrospect, Bloodsworth's convictions were somewhat surprising. As a young man, he had led a traditional and unremarkable life on Maryland's Eastern Shores, fishing, trapping, hunting, and crabbing, like many boys his age. His career in the U.S. Marine Corps was similarly unremarkable, marked only by a previously unknown prowess in the discus throw, a sport in which he hoped to compete further after being discharged from the Marines. Bloodsworth had no convictions on his record, no history of trouble with the law, and no connection with the murdered girl. Nonetheless, he entered prison with no hope of parole and no likelihood of ever again being a free man.

That scenario began to change, however, in 1992. Centurion Ministries of Princeton, New Jersey, an organization devoted to obtaining freedom for men and women falsely convicted of crimes, contacted Bloodsworth about the possibility of using a new investigative technique—*DNA fingerprinting*—in reconsidering evidence collected at the scene of the 1984 crime. DNA fingerprinting is a method by which the DNA pattern of an individual is compared against DNA from blood, semen, or other bodily materials collected at the scene of a crime. Since every person's DNA pattern is unique (except in the case of identical twins), a DNA fingerprint match is as close to an absolute identification as forensic scientists are likely to achieve.

Nearly a year after Centurion Ministries initiated the analysis of DNA samples taken from Bloodsworth and semen found on the murder victim's clothing, investigators at the Federal Bureau of Investigation (FBI) announced that the samples did not match. Bloodsworth could not have committed the crime for which he was convicted. On June 28, 1994, he was released from prison, and 18 months later, he received a full pardon by Maryland governor Donald Schaefer. The state awarded Bloodsworth $300,000 in compensation, or about $90 a day for each of his 3,247 days of wrongful confinement.

An Introduction to DNA

For more than a century, forensic scientists have relied heavily on the use of digital fingerprints—that is, prints formed by skin patterns on people's fingertips—as being the most certain method for identifying the perpetrator of a crime. Although no scientific evidence exists for the belief, fingerprint analysis is based on the *assumption* that no two individuals have exactly the same set of digital fingerprints. From time to time, that assumption has been contested in the courts, but judges tend to reject such arguments, and fingerprint evidence continues to be a powerful evidentiary tool for law enforcement officials.

Over the last two decades, a new analytical tool has been developed. It is based on variations in a person's DNA that can be broadly compared to differences in the fingerprint patterns of various individuals. Emphasizing this similarity, the new tool has been called DNA fingerprinting.

Many scientists suggest that this term is misleading or imprecise. In the case of digital fingerprinting, an analyst always has a complete set of data with which to work: all of the ridges, whorls, loops, stripes, and other distinctive characteristics on (usually) all 10 of a person's fingers. There are no missing data in a digital fingerprint. By contrast, an investigator has access to only a limited amount of any one person's DNA. As the discussion that follows explains, one person's DNA consists of billions of variable units (*base pairs*), only a small fraction of which, for practical reasons, can actually be examined. Because of this difference with the data available in digital fingerprinting, experts often suggest the term *DNA typing* or *DNA profiling* for the comparable analytical technique with DNA.

DNA is an abbreviation for the term *deoxyribonucleic acid,* a group of biochemical compounds found in the cells of nearly all living organisms. These compounds carry the genetic code that tells cells what functions they are to perform; thus they are arguably the most essential of all biochemical molecules. They also provide the mechanism by which this information is transmitted from generation to generation.

As shown in the diagram on page 134, a DNA molecule consists of two long strands wrapped around each other in a geometric conformation known as a double helix. The two strands are bonded loosely to each other by means of hydrogen bonds between adjacent units on each strand. The long, spaghettilike strands that make up DNA consist of repeating units known as *nucleotides.* Each nucleotide consists of three units: the sugar deoxyribose, a phosphate group, and one of four nitrogen bases. Two of the four nitrogen bases present in DNA, cytosine and thymine, are derivatives of the nitrogen base called pyrimidine, and two, adenine and guanine, are derivatives of the base known as purine.

Two nucleotide units can bond to each other to form a dinucleotide; three can bond to form a trinucleotide; four, to form a tetranucleotide;

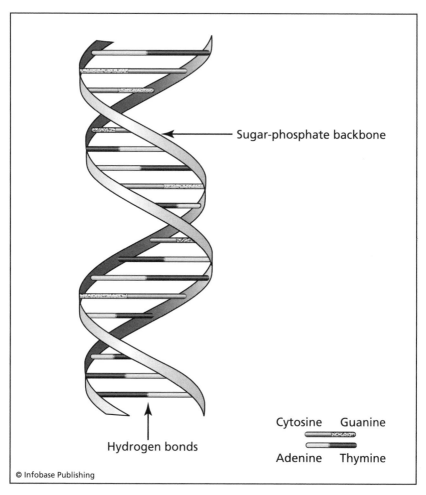

Sugar-phosphate backbone

Hydrogen bonds

Cytosine   Guanine

Adenine   Thymine

© Infobase Publishing

Structure of a DNA molecule

and so on. A single strand of DNA consists of many hundreds or thousands of nucleotides bonded to each other, a polynucleotide. In nature, the reaction of two nucleotides with each other is catalyzed by an enzyme called DNA polymerase. DNA polymerase is one member of a class of enzymes, the *polymerases,* that catalyze the addition of a subunit to a polymer.

In a DNA molecule, the two complementary strands are arranged with the sugar-phosphate backbone of the strand on the outside of the double helix, and the projecting nitrogen bases facing inward, adjacent to each other. These bases are not arranged randomly; they are paired according to a specific chemical rule: A purine base may align itself with a pyrimidine base only, and vice versa. That is, the only pairings of nitrogen bases permitted are those in which a guanine (G) on one strand is aligned with a cytosine (C) on the opposite strand and those in which an adenine (A) on one strand is matched with a thymine (T) on the opposite strand. Only these pairings permit the formation of the hydrogen bonds that stabilize the double helix and allow it to exist. The association of two nitrogen bases, one on each strand of a DNA molecule, is called a base pair. A typical DNA molecule contains about 3 billion base pairs.

Chemistry Explains Biology

Since the 1950s, scientists have discovered that the chemical structure of DNA determines an organism's biological form and function. In other words, they have learned that essentially all biological phenomena, such as growth, development, and reproduction, can be explained on the basis of chemical reactions as completely as can nonbiological phenomena, such as rusting and combustion.

Consider the process of inheritance as an example. For well over a century, biologists have understood the general rules that determine how certain traits are transmitted from generation to generation. The most fundamental of these rules are often known as the Mendelian laws, after the Austrian monk Gregor Mendel (1822–84), who carried out the original experiments on which they are based. These rules make use of certain units, called *genes,* that are presumed to be present in an organism's cells and that are passed down in some way from parent to offspring. But, for more than a century, biologists had no idea as to what a gene actually was. It remained a convenient and highly useful code word for the unit of inheritance.

Scientists now know precisely what a gene is: It is a sequence of nucleotides on a DNA molecule, like the one shown below.

-G-C-C-C-T-A-T-T-G-T-A-C-G-T-T-A-A-C-G-G-G-C-T-C-T-
-C-G-G-G-A-T-A-A-C-A-T-G-C-A-A-T-T-G-C-C-C-G-A-G-A-

One might say that the sequence of base pairs shown in this diagram represents a gene—except that the sequence shown is much too short. A single gene consists of tens or hundreds of thousands of base pairs, a structure that is not easily shown on one page.

One of the great accomplishments of modern science has been the elucidation of the human genome, the complete set of genes found in the human organism. Scientists have now determined the location and chemical structure of virtually all of the genes present in human cells, a total of somewhere between 30,000 and 40,000 genes. "Locating" a gene means locating the chromosome on which a gene is found and its position on that chromosome relative to other genes. The position of a gene on a chromosome is known as its *locus.*

In the process of recording the human genome, researchers have also found a chemical explanation for the existence of alleles. The term *allele,* like gene, was introduced by biologists to explain the fact that genetic traits often have two or more manifestations. That is, a person may be right-handed or left-handed (or, occasionally, ambidextrous). He may have blue eyes, hazel eyes, green eyes, or eyes of some other color. She may have blond, red, black, or brown hair, or hair of some other color. The presence of two or more forms of a genetic trait was said to be due to the fact that the gene controlling a particular physical characteristic could exist in two or more forms, or alleles.

Formerly, the word *allele* expressed a condition that scientists observed but could not account for. Today we know that alleles are nucleotide sequences (genes) that have different base-pair sequences. If a particular gene or genetic marker has many base-pair variations, it is said to be *polymorphic* ("many forms"). (A *genetic marker,* or, simply, marker, is any portion of a DNA molecule with a clearly defined genetic characteristic. It may or may not be a specific gene.)

Polymorphisms may occur in either of two forms: as variations in a nucleotide sequence or variations of nucleotide length. The diagram below shows three polymorphic forms (alleles) of a gene in which the third base pair from the left varies.

-A-A-C-A-G-T-T-A-C-G-
-T-T-G-T-C-A-A-T-G-C-

-A-A-T-A-G-T -T -A-C-G-
-T -T-A-T -C-A-A-T -G-C-

-A-A-A-A-G-T -T -A-C-G-
-T -T -T -T -C-A-A-T -G-C-

Length variations consist of DNA segments in which leading and trailing units are identical, but the segments enclosed between these units consist of differing base-pair segments. These base-pair segments are identical in structure but variable in length. The diagram below shows two polymorphisms of this kind. Notice that the first polymorphism contains four base-pairs repetitions, or *tandem repeats,* while the second polymorphism contains three tandem repeats. The tandem repeats are indicated in alternating degrees of shading. Tandem repeats that contain a relatively small number of repeated segments—usually two to five base pairs—are known as *short tandem repeats,* or STRs.

-G-C-T-A-T-C-G-C-T-A-T-C-G-C-T-A-T-C-G-C-T-A-T-C-
-G-C-T-A-T-C-G-C-T-A-T-C-G-C-T-A-T-C-

One erroneous impression that the above diagram may suggest is that DNA is a static molecule, a molecule in which nucleotides and their components are essentially fixed in space. That picture is misleading because DNA molecules, like all molecules, are constantly in motion, vibrating, rotating, and, most important, changing their physical and chemical compositions.

For example, DNA molecules are constantly in the process of replicating themselves. Each individual strand of a DNA molecule has the capacity to make an exact and faithful copy of itself, resulting eventually in the formation of two DNA molecules that are identical to the original DNA molecule. At the beginning of this process, DNA molecules unravel and separate at some locations, changing from a helical to a linear shape. Hydrogen bonds break, allowing the two strands of which DNA is made to separate. At this point, each of the DNA strands selects nucleotides from a supply in the cell to begin making a new strand that is complementary to the existing strand. Eventually, two new strands are formed, each complementary to the original strand from which it was produced. When the process of replication is finished, two DNA molecules exist, each an exact copy of the original DNA molecule from which they were formed.

The changes that take place during replication are made possible by a number of specialized enzymes that catalyze the breaking of bonds (the *lyases*) and the reconstruction of bonds (the *ligases*). Those enzymes that operate specifically on DNA molecules are known as DNA lyases and DNA ligases. Scientists have now identified many of these enzymes, manufactured them synthetically in the laboratory, and used them to manipulate DNA for a variety of purposes, including DNA typing.

Applications of DNA Testing

Variations in DNA are probably the single most reliable measure of genetic diversity. Organisms whose DNA differ dramatically have the greatest physical and biological diversity, while those whose DNA differ only moderately are relatively similar in their physical and biological characteristics. For example, scientists have determined that humans and yeast have about 46 percent of their genes in common. That is not much of a gene match, and there are certainly few similarities in physical and biological characteristics between the two organisms. Humans and fruit flies share between 60 and 70 percent of their genes; humans and dogs, about 75 percent; humans and mice, about 99 percent; and humans and chimpanzees and gorillas, about 99.4 percent. By comparison, all humans share about 99.5 percent of their genes with each other.

Today a complete or partial DNA map is available for a number of species, including yeasts, dogs, mice, chimpanzees, gorillas, and humans. Such maps show the locations (or *loci;* singular, *locus*) of genes as well as their nucleotide composition. These DNA maps are now available online for many species. For example, the human genome map can be found online at http://mgc.nci.nih.gov.

Scientists now believe that the human genome contains about 80,000 distinct genes. Each of these genes contains several thousand nucleotides. In addition to the genes that have been identified in the human genome, DNA maps also show regions within a DNA molecule that lie *between* genes, long nucleotide strings that have no known function. Such sequences are sometimes known as *junk DNA*. Junk DNA may make up as much as 97 percent of the total human genome, although it constitutes a much smaller portion of the genome of other species, such as the mustard weed, with about 11 percent junk DNA; the common housefly, about 3 percent junk DNA; and the pufferfish, nearly 0 percent junk DNA.

The availability of DNA maps makes possible a number of applications, including some of interest to a relatively small number of researchers and others of considerable practical value to many scientists and other professionals. For example, evolutionary biologists are interested in discovering how various species are related to each other and, therefore, what their evolutionary histories may be. If one could show, for instance, that 99 percent of the DNA in humans and raccoons were identical, then one might conclude that the two species are closely related to each other and that they evolved along similar paths through history.

The basis for this conclusion is that DNA is normally transmitted conservatively (without error) from parent to offspring. The DNA in an organism's cells is usually identical to that found in the cells of its parents' bodies. That general rule is violated only when *mutations* occur. A mutation is a change in DNA sequence caused by a burst of energy (such as X-rays), certain chemicals, or other factors. For example, a photon of radiation might strike a DNA molecule, rupture a bond within a nucleotide, and cause a change in nucleotide sequence.

Such mutations are thought to occur at the rate of about 2–4 percent per million years. That is, every million years, an average of two to four out of 100 base pairs on a DNA molecule will have mutated. Thus, the greater the number of different base pairs in the DNA of two species, the longer it has been since the two species have stopped interbreeding and become distinct species.

No close relationship between the DNA of humans and raccoons has been found. By contrast, there is a great similarity in the DNA of humans, gorillas, chimpanzees, and other apes. That result is hardly surprising, since other evidence has already demonstrated a close evolutionary relationship among humans and the apes.

Another field in which DNA testing has found application is wildlife biology. The protection of endangered species, for example, depends on knowing as much as possible about the behavior of these species in the wild and then doing whatever is necessary to protect their survival. In the past, the studies needed to learn about animal behavior were often invasive and disruptive. Researchers often had to anesthetize an animal with a dart gun and attach a collar or tag with a radio transmitter. Signals from the transmitter allowed researchers to track the animal, but the effect on the animal's normal behavior was sometimes impossible to estimate.

Now researchers can study animal behavior using DNA testing with little or no disruption of the animal's normal behaviors. For example, scientists can collect fur, hair, feathers, blood, feces, and other materials left behind by animals to determine the number, sex, age, location, migration pattern, and other characteristics of animals.

DNA testing can also be used to identify plant and animal life taken illegally by poachers. For example, logging is prohibited by law in some areas in order to protect certain endangered plant species. Individuals who violate such laws can be identified by examining DNA samples of trees and other plants found in their possession. If these DNA samples match similar samples taken from endangered species, the individuals are presumed to have taken those trees or plants illegally.

The first and one of the best-known fields in which DNA typing was used is paternity testing. Although it is always clear who the mother of a child is, there is sometimes a question as to who the child's father is. That information is often important for legal reasons, for instance, to determine the man who is legally responsible for a child's upbringing and/or financial support.

The DNA argument for paternity is simple. It is based on the fact that DNA is passed on conservatively (without change) from generation to generation. Thus, a child's DNA is some mixture of both parents' DNA. The first step in using DNA to establish paternity, then, is to establish DNA patterns for child and mother, both of which are easily obtained. The mother's DNA pattern can then, by some mechanism, be "subtracted from" the child's DNA pattern. The DNA that is left from that process must have come from the father's DNA pattern. That pattern can be compared to DNA samples taken from individuals who are presumed or suspected to be the father to determine whether a match exists. The presence or absence of a match confirms or rules out a man as the father of the child.

This method was first used in 1985 by the English scientist Alec Jeffreys (1950–), then at Leicester University in the United Kingdom. Jeffreys had just discovered a method for comparing the DNA collected from two different sources, a method that came to be called *restriction fragment length polymorphism* (RFLP). He was asked to determine the paternity of a boy living in Ghana who wished to emigrate to Great Britain, where his mother was then living. According to British law, the boy could be permitted to enter the country only if he could prove that he was a blood relative of an English citizen, in this case, his mother.

Jeffreys proposed to compare the boy's DNA with that of his presumptive mother (to confirm the maternal component of his DNA) and that of the woman's other children (to confirm the paternal component of the boy's DNA). The latter test was necessary because the boy's father could not be found and, therefore, could not provide a DNA sample directly.

When all DNA samples had been collected and analyzed, Jeffreys reported that the evidence was conclusive: The boy's DNA matched that taken from the presumed mother and her children. No DNA from the father was needed to prove his paternity, Jeffreys explained, because his DNA "fingerprint" could be deduced in the DNA of his mother's other children, the boy's siblings.

Forensic DNA Typing

DNA typing is clearly a powerful tool with numerous applications. In forensic science, it is used for the identification of individuals accused of rape, murder, and other violent crimes. Such applications are possible because DNA in such crimes is usually available from three essential sources: the victim; the perpetrator of the crime; and evidence left behind at the scene of the crime, such as blood, semen, hair, or other biological materials. Forensic DNA typing generally

◁ SIR ALEC JEFFREYS (1950–   ) ▷

Discoveries in science are seldom due entirely to the work of a single individual. More often, many researchers studying a common problem make important contributions to major breakthroughs. Such was the case in the 1980s with the basic procedures used in DNA fingerprinting. As early as 1980, Ray White and his colleagues at the University of Utah had discovered the presence of structures known as variable number tandem repeats (VNTRs) in DNA molecules. VNTRs play a critical role in one of the two major techniques used in DNA typing, restriction fragment length polymorphisms (RFLP). But it took the ingenuity and creativity of British scientist Alec Jeffreys to see how the work of White and other researchers could be utilized in the development of DNA typing.

Alec John Jeffreys was born in Oxford, England, on January 9, 1950. He was educated at Stopsley, Luton, Infant and Junior Schools, and then at Luton Grammar School (1961–66) and Luthon Sixth Form College (1966–68). He attended Merton College, Oxford, where he studied biochemistry from 1968 to 1972. In 1975, he was awarded his Ph.D. in human genetics by the University of Oxford. From 1975 to 1977, he worked as a postdoctoral student at the University of Amsterdam. After completing his postdoctoral studies, Jeffreys accepted an appointment as lecturer in the Department of Genetics at the University of Leicester.

Jeffreys's move to Leicester marked a new beginning in his research program. At Amsterdam, he had worked on the cloning of mammalian genes, without much success. When he arrived at Leicester, he decided on a new line of work: analyzing structural variations in genes and the effects these variations have in inheritance. One of the first discoveries arising from this research was the existence of restriction fragment length polymorphisms,

involves the comparison of these three kinds of DNA, as shown in the diagram on page 144.

DNA typing can determine conclusively (1) whether evidence at the crime scene, such as blood, hair, or other biological materials, came from the victim or, if not, (2) whether it came from some other known or unknown individual. If an individual is suspected of the crime and can supply DNA for analysis, an investigator can then compare that DNA with DNA present in the evidence to determine

which were to form the basis of one of the two primary methods of DNA typing used today. In 1985, Jeffreys was asked to use DNA typing to determine the paternity of a young man who wished to emigrate from Ghana to the United Kingdom. In the same year, he assisted a rape and murder investigation by police in the West Midlands. In both instances, DNA typing provided key evidence. The forensic importance of Jeffreys's discovery had been demonstrated beyond question.

Jeffreys has remained at Leicester since 1977, holding the posts of Lister Institute Research Fellow (1982–91), reader in genetics (1984–87), professor of genetics (1987–   ), Royal Society Wolfson Research Professor (1991–   ), and Howard Hughes International Research Scholar (1993–99). He is currently professor of genetics at Leicester.

Jeffreys has been awarded a host of honors, including election to the Royal Society (1986), the Colworth Medal for Biochemistry of the Biochemical Society (1985), the Linnean Bicentenary Medal for Zoology of the Linnean Society (1987), the Carter Medal of the Clinical Genetics Society (1987), the Davy Medal of the Royal Society (1987), the Allen Award of the American Society of Human Genetics (1992), the Gold Medal for Zoology of the Linnean Society of London (1994), and the Albert Einstein World of Science Award of the World Cultural Council (1996). In 1994, Jeffreys was knighted by Queen Elizabeth II for his services to science and technology. In 2004, he was awarded D.Sc. by the University of Leicester and the Royal Medal by the Royal Society.

Jeffreys is married with two daughters. He says that his pastimes include walking, postal history, movies, reading "rubbish novels," and surfing ("the wet kind, not Internet").

whether it matches. If the match *does* exist, the suspect is almost certainly responsible for the crime. If *no* match exists, the suspect is almost certainly not responsible for the crime.

The essential scientific fact that makes this kind of analysis possible is that the *biological origin* of the DNA obtained from any one of the three sources is irrelevant. That is, the victim's DNA sample may have come from a drop of blood; the evidentiary DNA from a flake of skin; and the suspect's DNA from a single hair. The DNA found in

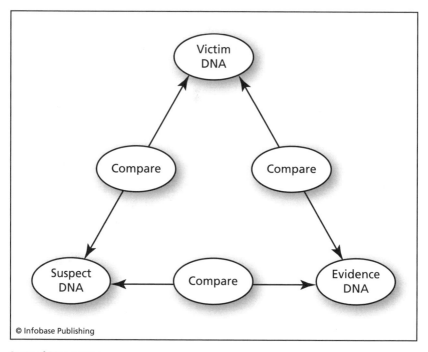

Basis of DNA typing

person's body is the same in all of the 75 trillion cells that make up his or her body. DNA taken from blood cells, skin cells, semen cells, or any other kind of cell is identical. If the DNA from a drop of blood from one source, a flake of skin from a second source, and a hair from a third source all match, they must all have come from the same source.

Suppose that an analysis of blood taken from a crime scene and blood drawn from a suspect has been completed. And suppose that analysis shows a "match" of DNA patterns at all of the loci examined. Can it be said that the suspect is responsible for the crime?

That question is far more difficult to answer than it might at first appear. Some problems associated with the question are suggested by the use of quotation marks around "match." One interpretation of that term might be that every base pair in the suspect's DNA is identical with every base pair in the evidentiary DNA. But, of course, that kind of match could never be observed, because no DNA typing ever examines *every* base pair in a person's DNA. Indeed, typing looks at only a minute fraction of all possible base pairs. To say that two samples "match," then, means only that any differences in the two DNA samples that *do* exist or *may* exist have not been found.

To increase one's confidence in the "match," an analyst would like to increase the number of loci studied. The more loci at which no differences are found, the greater his or her confidence that the two DNA samples are alike (similar or identical). Any trustworthy method of DNA typing, therefore, tests loci with as many different variations as possible.

Other reasons exist to question the strength of a "match." For example, while it is possible that the DNA sequences tested *were* identical for the sample and the suspect, it is also possible that the suspect and some other person shared the same DNA sequence *at the loci being tested.* Such results might be obtained for members of the same family because blood relatives are likely to share a greater portion of their DNA with each other than they do with strangers. Brothers and sisters, cousins and nephews and nieces, grandparents and third cousins are all more closely related to each other than they are to neighbors, coworkers, and friends; therefore, they have DNA that is more similar to each other than it is to nonrelatives. A DNA sample that "matches" that of a suspect might, under some circumstances, "match" that of the suspect's brother, cousin, or aunt.

Thus "matching" of DNA samples is never a matter of certainty, an issue of "yes, they match" versus "no, they do not match." Instead, matching is a question of probability. The question a forensic scientist usually has to answer is, given the number and character of loci being tested, the type of test performed, the possibility of sample contamination, the possibility of laboratory error, and other factors, what is the likelihood that DNA from a piece of evidence is the same as DNA from a suspect?

That question is one of the most difficult and contentious of all issues raised by DNA typing. Whole books have been written in an effort to answer it in a way that will be acceptable to the legal system, the scientific community, and the general public. These books make use of sophisticated statistical analyses to decide how a host of factors involved in DNA typing will affect the likelihood that some specific correlation is likely to occur by chance. Some decision must then be made as to what an acceptable level of probability is, how likely it is that an observed match actually connects a suspect with a crime.

The fundamental question is what level of probability is needed to make a reasonable connection between DNA from evidence and DNA from a suspect. Is the probability that the match occurs by chance only one time in 100 conclusive? Or would it be necessary to have a probability of one out of 1,000 or one out of a million? What probability *could* be regarded as convincing?

The Federal Bureau of Investigation (FBI) has argued that a reasonable probability level is about one in 100 billion (one in 10^{11}). That is, if two DNA matches can be shown to occur with a likelihood of only about 1 out of 10^{11}, then there is a 99 percent chance that the suspect is the only person in the United States who could have committed the crime in question.

At first glance, that standard seems high. Is it possible to obtain matches with this degree of probability in the kind of DNA typing that is usually carried out? The answer is yes, it can be done. Indeed, it is a commentary on the power of DNA typing that low probabilities such as these can, under the proper circumstances, be obtained. Some authorities disagree with the FBI's conclusion and/or the calculations by which it was obtained. In spite of this controversy, a consensus appears to have evolved in which some probability level close to that suggested by the FBI will be accepted by a majority of forensic scientists.

On the other hand, debates about the relative value of one in 10 billion versus one in 1 trillion probabilities may be reaching a level of academic absurdity that may not be relevant in practice: They may not convince judges and juries of the value of DNA evidence. As noted criminologist Dr. David Stoney has said, in referring to the value of digital fingerprints, "individualization cannot be proven; we can only become convinced of it." In the last analysis, then, it may require some combination of strong mathematical analysis that determines probabilities with a "sense of conviction" that will determine the guilt or innocence of many accused men and women.

Procedures for DNA Typing

Two technologies are currently in general use for the analysis of DNA patterns: restriction fragment length polymorphisms (RFLP) and *polymerase chain reaction* (PCR). In either case, a number of steps are usually necessary before the analysis of a DNA sample can be initiated. First, the DNA sample must be removed from the material on which it was deposited (a shirt, carpet, floor, victim's skin, or other body part, for example). It must then be cleaned and separated from non-DNA materials that would contaminate the analysis. It must also be examined to determine the amount of DNA present and its integrity, meaning the amount of DNA that remains intact. Like most biological materials, DNA degrades over time. That is, a single DNA molecule tends to break apart into two, three, four, and eventually many parts. The type of analysis that can be used on any given DNA sample depends on both the integrity of the DNA and the amount available for testing.

Organic extraction is perhaps the simplest and most common method for removing a DNA sample from the material on which it has been deposited. In this procedure, a piece of the material is cut from the whole object (a garment or carpet, for example) and added to a flask containing an organic solvent—usually phenol, chloroform, isoamyl alcohol, or some combination of these solvents. The flask is then warmed, increasing the rate at which cells in the sample are released from the material and dissolved in the solvent.

When removal of the biological material from the sample appears complete, the cells obtained are transferred to a second flask and mixed with another reagent, such as EDTA (ethylenediaminetetraacetic acid), sodium dodecyl sulfate, or tris[hydroxymethane]aminomethane. This reagent causes the lysis (rupture) of cells, releasing pure DNA, which can then be concentrated and collected for further study.

Other methods of separation are also available. For example, the DNA-impregnated sample can be added to a flask containing Chelex beads. Chelex is a resin made of styrene divinylbenzene, to which are attached two iminodiacetate ions. The iminodiacetate ions act as chelating groups; that is, they appear to bind to the metal ions that are involved in the breakdown of DNA chains. The flask is then heated to boiling. During the boiling process, cells break open (undergo lysis) and release their DNA to the surrounding solution. Non-DNA materials bind to the Chelex beads, while DNA itself remains in solution. Removal of the beads leaves behind a relatively pure solution of DNA, which can then be dried and used for analysis. The Chelex bead method is most frequently used with small samples that will be analyzed by the PCR method.

The presence of sperm cells on a piece of evidence may complicate the extraction procedures just described. Sperm cells are more resistant to attack than other cells, requiring a modified approach to extraction. In this approach, the piece of evidence containing both sperm and nonsperm cells is exposed to organic extraction, as already described. That extraction removes both types of cells from the material on which they are deposited. The resulting mixture is then centrifuged, causing it to separate into a clear solution containing nonsperm DNA and a clump of material at the bottom of the centrifuge tube containing precipitated sperm DNA. The two components can then be separated and treated with distinct reagents suitable for the lysis of each type of cell.

The next step in preparing for DNA analysis is *quantitation,* determining the amount of human DNA present in the sample. The reason quantitation is necessary is that DNA samples are often contaminated with DNA from nonhuman sources, such as DNA from bacteria. Bacterial DNA does not interfere with the DNA analysis itself, but it may provide a false indication of the amount of DNA present, and this measure is essential in deciding what kind of DNA test to perform and how to carry out that test.

A common method for determining the quantity of human DNA is called the *slot-blot* test. In slot-blot testing, a drop of one or more samples to be tested is attached to a strip of nylon cloth. A series of drops containing DNA standards, each containing some known amount of DNA, is also attached to the nylon strip. Each standard drop contains some known amount of DNA. In the diagram on page 149, the column of lines at the left of the test strip contains samples of a known DNA. The other columns of lines contain DNA taken from samples collected from the victim, the crime scene, and/or the suspect.

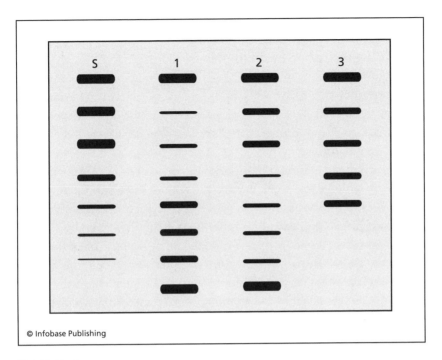

Slot-blot test

A drop of *DNA probe* is then added to each spot on the nylon strip. DNA probe is a chemical tool that consists of two parts. The first part is a short piece of synthetic DNA that will bind to a particular part of the human DNA present on the nylon strip. The second part of the probe is a "tag," a chemical group that is chemiluminescent; that is, it will emit light when treated with the appropriate reagent. The two most common reagents used in the tag are luminol (3-aminophthalhydrazide) in combination with horseradish peroxidase (HRP) and dioxethane in combination with the enzyme alkaline phosphatase (AP). In either case, the luminol or dioxethane emits visible light when it is stimulated by ultraviolet light, a process catalyzed by either HRP or AP. The DNA probes are allowed to bond with the spots on the nylon strip and then treated with the reagent. The spots then become visible as colored points on the nylon strip.

The intensity of the color produced in each position on the nylon strip provides a measure of the amount of human DNA present in each sample, compared with the standards present on the strip. Although estimates can be made visually of the quantity of human DNA present in each sample, a more precise measure can be obtained by making use of an automated colormetric system that measures the intensity of radiation emitted at each wavelength of light in the visible spectrum.

A second technique for assessing the amount of DNA present in a sample is called a yield gel. A yield gel consists of a solid platform (a support system; for example, a piece of plastic) covered with a thin layer of agarose gel, made by heating and then cooling agar, a colloidal extract of algae. A row of indentations (wells) runs parallel to the top of the platform. One or more samples are placed into each of these wells along with a number of standards. The standards consist of DNA samples of known size and complete integrity. An electrical potential is then applied to the agarose gel, drawing DNA fragments downward through the gel. After some period of time (usually less than an hour), the agarose gel is treated with the reagent ethidium bromide (EB). EB binds with double-stranded nucleic acids and fluoresces when exposed to ultraviolet light. The pattern of fluorescing spots on the agarose gel can then be photographed and/or analyzed by colorometric means to determine the amount of double-stranded DNA present.

The pattern formed in a yield gel also provides information about the integrity of DNA in a sample, because the larger a DNA molecule, the larger and more intense the spot of light it produces and the closer that spot is to its point of origin at the top of the gel. By contrast, a degraded piece of DNA produces a larger, less well-defined, less visually intense spot of light that has migrated downward from its point of origin to a greater degree. Because EB bonds only poorly with single-stranded DNA, severely degraded DNA consisting of such structures will be only poorly visible, or not visible at all. The advantage of a yield gel is that it provides evidence as to the integrity of the DNA sample, that is, the extent to which it has or has not been degraded. Its disadvantage is that it does not distinguish among DNA from a variety of species.

Methods of DNA Typing

Some of the steps involved in the two methods of DNA typing, RFLP and PCR, are similar, while others are quite different from each other.

The first DNA-typing technology to have been developed was restriction fragment length polymorphism (RFLP), initially worked out by Alec Jeffreys in 1985. This technology depends on the use of certain types of enzymes, known as *restriction enzymes,* that recognize and cut DNA at specific locations identified by characteristic base patterns. Many different restriction enzymes are now known. For example, the restriction enzyme known as AluI recognizes the following base pattern wherever it appears in a strand of DNA:

AGCT
TCGA

When it finds such a strand, it cuts the bonds at the middle of the pattern:

AG CT
TC GA

An example of the way in which AluI would operate on an extended strand of DNA is shown on page 152.

In theory, a number of different restriction enzymes could be used in this type of reaction. A list of all known restriction enzymes with their DNA targets is available online at http://www.molecular-workshop.com/data/endonucleases.html. In practice, however, researchers have chosen to focus on a small number of such enzymes. The most popular enzyme in the United States is the enzyme HaeIII, and the most popular in Europe is HinfI. HaeIII recognizes the base pattern, which it cuts at the middle of the pattern:

GG CC
CC GG

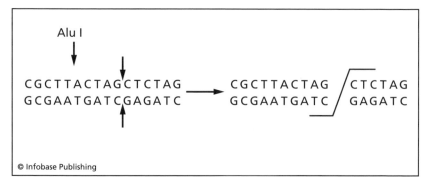

Action of restriction enzyme AluI

By contrast, the enzyme HinfI recognizes the following base pattern (where N represents any nitrogen base), which it cuts after the initial base pair:

G A NTC
C T NAG

The first step in an RFLP analysis is to combine in an incubation tube the DNA sample to be tested and a carefully determined amount of the chosen restriction enzyme. The incubation tube is then maintained at an elevated temperature for a period of time, usually overnight. This process presumes that the restriction enzyme will find and cut all of the distinctive segments of DNA for which it has been selected. When this has occurred, the DNA is said to have been *digested.* Confirmatory tests are generally conducted after incubation to ensure that complete digestion has occurred. If it has not, some artificially large segments will remain, masking the true number of short tandem repeats (STRs) in the sample. If the DNA sample is not completely digested, additional restriction enzyme or an extended incubation time may be necessary.

Once digestion is complete, the incubation tube contains a number of alleles with identical initial and concluding base-pair patterns. These alleles differ only in the number of repeating units between the beginning and ending base pairs, or length polymorphisms. The number of alleles may be quite large; indeed, DNA segments are chosen for cutting *because* they show so much variability.

The next step in the process is to determine the size of the STR segments that have been produced during incubation. The technique used to do so is called electrophoresis. The process described here is similar to gel electrophoresis. First, the digested DNA is added to a well at one end of a plate covered with agarose. (In actual practice, a number of DNA samples are added to a row of wells in the plate. These wells may contain DNA samples from one or more suspects, one or more victims, and evidence collected at the crime scene, as well as DNA segments used as references in typing.)

Next, an electrical charge is applied to the agarose-coated plate such that the upper end of the plate (the well) carries a negative charge and the lower end has a positive charge. This arrangement is selected because DNA fragments carry an overall negative charge and will be pulled out of their wells and through the agarose to the bottom of the plate. The *rate* at which DNA fragments move differs, however, depending on their sizes. The smaller the DNA fragment, the more rapidly it moves through the agarose gel, while the larger the fragment, the more slowly it moves.

After some period of time (a few hours), the lightest DNA fragments have reached the bottom of the plate, and separation is presumed to be complete. The pattern of fragments formed as DNA is pulled out of each well by the electrical potential used is called a *lane*. The diagram on page 154 shows how lanes are formed during the process of electrophoresis.

At this point, the DNA fragments are denatured. *Denaturation* converts DNA fragments from a double-stranded form into a single-stranded form. To accomplish this, the tester adds first hydrochloric acid (HCl) and then sodium hydroxide (NaOH) to the gel. These two reagents break the hydrogen bonds between the two complementary strands of DNA, converting them to single strands. The strands are then extracted from the gel by placing a sheet of nylon and a sheet of absorbent material, such as a paper towel, on top of the gel. This process is known as *Southern blotting*. Single-stranded DNA fragments migrate upward from the gel, into the nylon, where they are fixed in position.

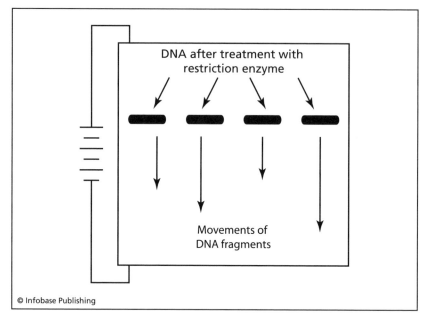

© Infobase Publishing

Separation of DNA fragments by electrophoresis

At this point, the DNA fragments on the nylon platform are not visible. To make them visible, the investigator adds DNA probes, small fragments of synthetic DNA that have been designed to bond with base-pair sequences known to be present in the STR sections under study. For example, suppose that an analyst knows that the STR section under investigation contains the base sequence ATCTTCAT. He or she can synthesize a DNA probe with the complementary sequence TAGAAGTA. When added to the nylon platform, the probe would "look for" and bind to all ATCTTCAT segments present.

Next, the investigator uses either a radioisotope or a chemical group that emits visible light under radiation to reveal the presence of the newly formed combination of DNA fragment plus DNA probe. One might, for example, use a radioisotope of one of the elements (such as phosphorus 32) present in the DNA probe that was synthesized. In this case, the location of all fragment-probe complexes can be determined by placing a photographic plate on top of the platform. Radiation emitted by each radioactive probe segment then "takes its own picture," producing an *autoradiograph,* or *autorad.* The

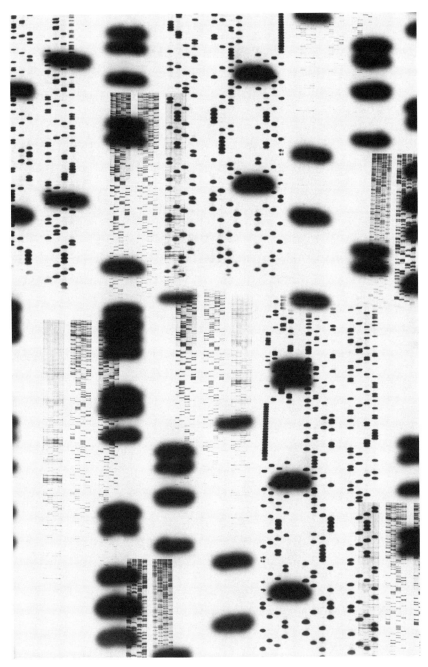

An autoradiogram of DNA sequences obtained in an RFLP test. (Alfred Pasieka/Photo Researchers, Inc.)

photograph on page 155 depicts an autoradiograph formed in this way. In the second approach, the DNA probe is attached to an additional chemical group that emits visible light when stimulated by radiation (such as ultraviolet light). In this case, the presence of each fragment-probe complex is revealed by the glow it produces when exposed to such radiation.

In either case, a permanent record of the location of each DNA fragment can be obtained. This record is comparable to the UPC bar code by which many products are priced today. Each "bar" on the DNA autorad represents an STR fragment of some size, from largest to smallest in moving down the sheet. Any given autorad contains a number of columns (or *lanes*). One or more of these lanes shows patterns from known standards (such as all the alleles possible within this locus); another may show DNA taken from a victim; a third, DNA from an evidentiary sample; and a fourth (and so on) from one or more suspects.

The analysis and interpretation of autorads like this one are generally quite difficult, depending to some degree on an individual's ability to pick out and recognize significant patterns. One trend today in DNA typing is toward the development of mechanical devices that are able to detect and match radiograms or color spots from various sources to provide more reliable comparisons of different DNA samples. Even when those comparisons have been made, however, questions about their statistical significance (as discussed earlier in this chapter) remain to be answered.

The second major method used in DNA analysis, polymerase chain reaction (PCR), is an adaptation of a common reaction involving DNA that occurs in nature: replication. Recall from the discussion earlier in this chapter that replication occurs when the two strands of which DNA are made uncoil and separate. Each of the exposed single strands then acts as a template from which a new strand of DNA is made. After replication is complete, two molecules of DNA, both identical to the original parent molecule, have been formed.

The steps involved in a PCR reaction are shown in the diagram on page 157. The first step in this sequence, denaturation, mimics the first step in replication by forcing a DNA molecule to uncoil and separate into two single-stranded segments. Denaturation is accomplished simply by heating DNA to a relatively high temperature, about 94°C.

Next, two *DNA primers* are prepared synthetically. (A DNA primer is the same as a DNA probe in that it contains some sequence of base pairs designed to find and bond to some specific base-pair sequence of interest in the sample DNA. Two separate terms are used, however, because of the different ways in which they are used.) For example, a researcher may wish to replicate only one segment of a DNA molecule, one with the sequence

GCAGGCATCTAG

CGTCCGTAGATC

The primers needed, then, will contain base-pair patterns complementary to the beginning and end of the desired segments. In this case, one primer would contain the sequence CGTC, complementary to the beginning of one (the upper) strand, and the other primer would contain the sequence GTAG, complementary to the ending of

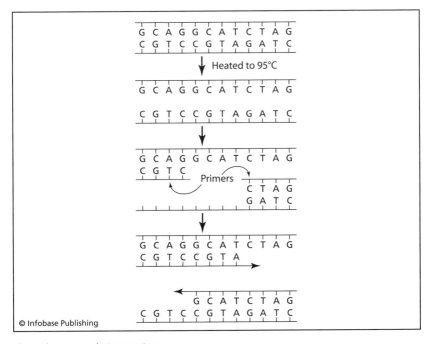

© Infobase Publishing

The polymerase chain reaction

the other (lower) strand. When the two primers are mixed with the denatured (single-stranded) DNA, they will bond at either end of the segment to be replicated, a process known as *annealing.*

Then the final step, known as *extension,* begins. Extension occurs when the units of which DNA is made—nucleotides—are carried into position and joined to single-stranded DNA by "building enzymes," as shown in the diagram. Building enzymes is an informal name for a group of enzymes more accurately known as *polymerases.* Polymerases are enzymes that join two or more molecular components to make one large unit. The polymerases used in the extension step of PCR are *DNA polymerases.*

In theory, any number of polymerases could be used during the extension phase of PCR. But only one is actually used in practice—the Taq polymerase, an enzyme that occurs naturally in bacteria found in hot springs and geysers. This enzyme, like the bacteria from which it comes, is able to survive high temperatures. It is used in PCR because it is not destroyed during denaturation when heat is used. As extension takes place, two new strands of DNA are formed, each identical to one of the original DNA strands. Four single strands of DNA, two complementary double strands, now exist.

The sequence of denaturation, annealing, and extension can then be repeated, resulting in the formation of four complete, double-stranded DNA strands, all identical to the original DNA. The process can be repeated again and again, each time doubling the number of identical DNA strands. The process of producing more and more samples of identical DNA is known as DNA *amplification.* In a typical application of the PCR analysis of a DNA segment, amplification may be repeated about 30 to 35 times, resulting in the formation of 10^{30} to 10^{35} (well over 100 million) copies of the original DNA.

One advantage of the PCR system is that amplification can be carried out at more than one locus at a time. That is, DNA primers can be designed to replicate a number of different loci at once, a process known as *multiplexing.* Multiplexing is what makes PCR a more powerful and more popular analytical tool for DNA typing than RFLP. Although the variability in any one locus is likely to be less than that for a locus used with RFLP, PCR can study a larger number of loci at one time, resulting in an overall greater *power of discrimination* (the ability to distinguish between any two individuals or events).

The product of PCR amplification is a mixture of DNA fragments with polymorphisms at a number of different loci. Identification of those DNA fragments involves a comparison of their characteristics against DNA taken from other sources, such as the victim or evidentiary material, and/or against certain standards, such as known alleles. This identification is carried out by analysis of either length polymorphisms or sequence polymorphisms, depending on the nature of the polymorphisms being examined. Analysis of length polymorphisms is generally similar to that for RFLP, although the process is often simpler and "cleaner" with PCR because a single, very pure segment of DNA is available with PCR but not necessarily with RFLP.

The product PCR is prepared for electrophoresis: It is loaded into a well on a platform containing polyacrylamide gel. Adjacent wells contain *allelic ladders* with which the sample(s) will eventually be compared. An allelic ladder is a set of DNA fragments of precise and known size that can be used to estimate the size of an unknown DNA fragment. A potential difference (voltage) is then applied to the platform, as in RFLP, and DNA fragments of various sizes migrate down the platform at different rates. Smaller fragments move more rapidly and reach the bottom of the platform first, while larger fragments migrate more slowly and tend to remain near the top of the platform. The bands formed in this process are then stained with silver nitrate and compared to the standard ladders and to other patterns formed on the platform. The product of this separation process is similar to the autorad depicted on page 155.

In one modification of this procedure, the PCR product is added to a capillary column containing liquid polyacrylamide. The separation produced by electrophoresis in the sample can then be compared directly with comparable tubes of known standards.

Sequence polymorphisms are usually analyzed by means of the *reverse dot-blot* procedure (also known as the sequence specific oligonucleotide test). This procedure makes use of commercially available test strips made of nylon to which are attached small oligonucleotides of known composition. An oligonucleotide is a molecule consisting of "many" (usually fewer than 25) nucleotide units bonded to each other. It is equivalent to the size and character of a DNA segment amplified by PCR methods. In fact, the coding of the oligonucleotide sequence is specifically designed to complement a portion of one such segment. If one of the DNA loci being tested by PCR contains the segment ATTCTTGTTCCAG, for example, then a comparable oligonucleotide probe will be designed with the complementary structure TAAGAACAAGGTC. A discrete probe for each locus tested by PCR is needed and is generally available.

The procedure for testing for a sequence polymorphism is shown in the diagram on page 161. The test strip contains a row of spots at which different oligonucleotides have been placed. Each oligonucleotide is marked for purposes of identification. The PCR product is added to each of the spots on the test strip. At any location where the product and the oligonucleotide match, a bond forms between the probe and the PCR product. Bonding occurs if, and only if, the oligonucleotide and DNA fragment match exactly, base for base.

DNA-oligonucleotide complexes that form are clear and colorless. A prior step in the testing procedure is necessary to make them visible. Namely, a molecule of biotin must be attached to the DNA fragment developed during PCR. Biotin is a member of the vitamin B complex family and is sometimes referred to as *vitamin H.*

After the PCR product has been added to the nylon test strip, a drop of a mixture of streptavidin (a protein) and horseradish peroxidase conjugate (HRP) is added to each oligonucleotide drop on the strip. Then a drop of the chemical tetramethylbenzidine (TMB) is also added to each oligonucleotide site.

The biotin that has been added to the PCR product tends to bond tightly with streptavidin. At the same time, the HRP associated with the streptavidin reacts with TMB to form a characteristic blue color. The blue HRP-TMB complex, bonded tightly to the DNA-biotin-streptavidin complex provides a vivid, simple, and obvious indication of where DNA fragments have bonded to the oligonucleotide. Because the structure of each oligonucleotide on the strip is known, the complementary structure of the attached DNA fragment is easily identified.

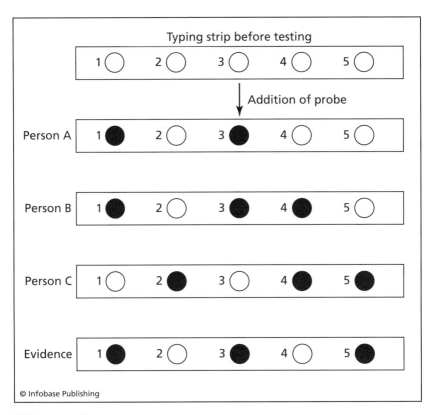

Typing strip before testing

Person A

Person B

Person C

Evidence

© Infobase Publishing

DNA typing strip

An application of the reverse dot-blot procedure is shown in the diagram on page 162. In this diagram, PCR samples from the victim (V), two suspects (S_1 and S_2), and two pieces of evidence (a drop of blood, B, and a sample of semen, S_e) are compared with two controls (C_+ and C_-). Notice that matches are obtained for the victim and the blood sample, for suspect 1 and the blood sample, and suspect 1 and the semen sample. An actual reverse dot-blot strip would contain additional measures that would strengthen any conclusions drawn from this test. Even based on this simplified example, however, it is clear that suspect 2 can be excluded from consideration as a perpetrator of this crime, while the evidence implicating suspect 1 is somewhat convincing. Again, statistical analysis would be needed to provide a numerical probability of this individual's involvement in the crime.

1	2	3	4	5	6	7
●		●		◐	●	●
			●		●	◐
	●		●	○	●	
			●		●	
			●		●	
●				◐		○
				●		

© Infobase Publishing

Reverse dot-blot test

Each DNA-typing technology uses its own approach and has its own strengths and weaknesses. For example, RFLP testing requires some minimum amount of relatively high molecular weight (HMW) DNA. The term *high molecular weight* means a fragment size of at least 20,000 to 25,000 base pairs. The amount of HMW DNA needed for a test varies according to the procedure used, but falls in the range of 10–50 nanograms (10^{-9}g).

By contrast, PCR technologies can be used with much shorter DNA strands, sometimes as small as a few hundred base pairs. They also require much smaller samples, often as little as 0.3 nanogram of DNA under the best of circumstances.

The greatest strength of RFLP is that it focuses on certain DNA loci with many (often hundreds) of variations. Thus, the analysis of only one or two loci may be sufficient to show significant differences between two DNA samples. The problem is that RFLP examines only one locus at a time before moving on to the next locus, making the process somewhat slow and laborious. In addition, RFLP is largely a manual, labor-intensive, time-consuming process that has been difficult to automate.

By contrast, PCR tends to use loci with less variability than does RFLP, resulting in a reduced power of discrimination for any given locus. But PCR has the ability to examine many loci simultaneously,

◄ KARY B. MULLIS (1944–) ►

The key problem facing any forensic scientist is to find a way of linking one particular individual with one specific crime. Criminologists have developed a number of techniques to accomplish this goal, ranging from fingerprinting to blood tests. No identification test has ever been so powerful and so widely accepted, however, as DNA typing. During the 1980s, two techniques for identifying a person on the basis of DNA tests were developed, restriction fragment length polymorphisms, by Alec Jeffreys, and polymerase chain reactions, by Kary Mullis.

Kary B. Mullis was born in Lenoir, North Carolina, on December 28, 1944. He attended Georgia Institute of Technology, from which he received his B.S. degree in chemistry in 1966. He then enrolled at the University of California at Berkeley (UCB), where he earned his Ph.D. in biochemistry in 1972. After graduation, Mullis remained at UCB as a lecturer in biochemistry for one year before taking a postdoctoral appointment in pediatric cardiology at the University of Kansas Medical School. In 1977, he began a two-year postdoctoral program in pharmaceutical chemistry at the University of California at San Francisco.

In 1979, Mullis was offered a position with the biotechnology company Cetus Corporation. He spent seven years there, working primarily on oligonucleotide synthesis. It was during this period that Mullis conceived of the method that has become known as polymerase chain reaction. That procedure was already well understood by chemists. It occurs naturally during the replication of DNA in cells, and researchers had succeeded in replicating the process in the laboratory. The problem they encountered, however, was that the high temperatures needed for denaturation of the DNA molecule destroyed the enzyme (DNA polymerase) needed for annealing. Mullis's great contribution was his suggestion of using DNA polymerase taken from thermophilic bacteria, which can withstand the heat used during denaturation. For his discovery, Cetus paid Mullis $10,000, an insignificant amount in view of the fact that the company later sold rights to the PCR process to Hoffman-LaRoche pharmaceutical company for $300 million. Mullis is now vice president and director of molecular biology for Burstein Technologies, located in Irvine, California.

In addition to the Nobel Prize, Mullis has been awarded the Japan Prize (1993), the Thomas A. Edison Award (1993), the California Scientist of the Year Award (1992), the National Biotechnology Award (1991), the R&D Scientist of the Year award (1991), and the Gairdner Award (1991). He was inducted into the Inventors Hall of Fame in 1998.

greatly increasing its *overall* power of discrimination. In addition, PCR has been automated, making its use faster and less expensive.

Whatever advantages RFLP may have had in the past, it now appears to be losing favor compared with PCR technologies. In fact, some authorities have predicted that the [RFLP] method is likely to disappear from active use in the near future.

Issues Involved in DNA Typing

DNA typing clearly provides a powerful analytical tool for forensic scientists. The ability to say with a probability of one out of a million or one out of a billion that a specific individual is or is not the perpetrator of a crime provides law enforcement officials with what may be the most useful tool they have ever had.

Despite what the preceding discussion might suggest, the development and use of DNA typing is not—and never has been—a simple and "clean" technology. This is one drawback of DNA typing. Another is the potential for invasion of privacy. The availability of DNA typing opens the door for a host of new programs and procedures in which governmental agencies might be able to collect personal information about an individual, store those data in huge databanks, and use it in (theoretically) whatever way they wanted.

Problems with the use of DNA typing in criminal cases became obvious soon after forensic scientists adopted the techniques. The first case in which RFLP was used, *State of Florida v. Tommy Lee Andrews* (1986), resulted in a hung jury when jurors were unable to agree whether DNA typing provided convincing proof of Andrews's guilt. Nonetheless, the courts *did* accept the validity of DNA typing both at the original trial and at the subsequent retrial, in which Andrews was found guilty.

Less than a year later, the first formal legal objection to the use of DNA evidence was raised in the case of the murder of a Bronx woman, Vilma Ponce, and her two-year-old daughter. A neighbor, Joseph Castro, was charged with the murders, partially because of a blood smear found on his watchband. The blood was later analyzed by scientists at a company called Lifecodes that specialized in RFLP testing. Those scientists issued a report saying that RFLP analysis proved conclusively that the blood on Castro's watchband matched that of the murdered woman.

Castro's attorneys questioned that conclusion. They asked for a review by four authorities in the field of DNA typing of Lifecode's procedures and interpretation of the evidence. The authorities found a number of problems with Lifecode's work. For one thing, they discovered that the DNA samples examined by Lifecodes had been contaminated by bacterial DNA, resulting in the formation of two extra bands in the RFLP pattern. Lifecodes scientists had incorrectly chosen to ignore those bands. Also, Lifecodes workers had carried out a statistical analysis of the typing results that, the four authorities decided, was incorrect and that greatly overestimated the probability of Castro having been the perpetrator of the crime.

Judge Gerald Sheindlin accepted the report of the four experts and declared the DNA evidence inadmissible. Although the prosecution had lost its most important single piece of evidence, Castro was convicted anyway on the basis of other evidence. He later confessed to the crime and admitted that the blood on his watchband was that of the victim.

After another 20 years of research and development, DNA-typing procedures are far more reliable than they were at the time of the Castro case. Dozens of individuals convicted of murder and rape have been cleared over the past two decades because of new data obtained as the result of DNA typing. Centurion Ministries alone has been responsible for the release of nearly three-dozen innocent people convicted of such crimes. At the same time, the guilt of many more individuals has been confirmed as the result of DNA testing.

One of the most controversial issues related to DNA typing is the possibility of developing large collections of DNA "fingerprints" of many individuals. Such *DNA databases* would be valuable because most individuals who commit a crime are repeat offenders. It is relatively rare that a person steals, assaults, rapes, or murders only once. Instead, individuals tend to commit the same or different offenses over and over again.

One way to increase the likelihood of catching a criminal, then, might be to collect DNA samples from anyone convicted of a crime and to store those samples in a central repository. DNA samples collected at some later crime scene could then be compared to those in the DNA database. Any matches found would reveal with high probability the perpetrator of that crime.

The first such database in the United States was established by the state of Virginia in 1989. Today every state in the Union maintains a DNA database for at least some types of crime, most commonly sexual offenses and murder. In 1994, the U.S. Congress authorized the creation of a National DNA Index System (NDIS) that would bring together the information stored in individual state databases. The system that was developed is now known as the Combined DNA Index System (CODIS). By the end of 1998, all 50 states had joined the CODIS, at least in principle. With this linkage, DNA "fingerprints" from more than 250,000 criminals became available to almost 100 public crime laboratories conducting DNA typing.

The problem was that, for two reasons, CODIS did not begin to function as quickly and as efficiently as many law enforcement officials had hoped. First, members' resources were unequal. Not every state and every forensic laboratory had the technology, the expertise, and/or the financial resources to collect, analyze, and record the DNA samples available to it. By one estimate, as many as 750,000 blood samples collected from convicts nationwide had yet to be analyzed and entered into state databases in 2001. Such technological problems will always exist, of course, preventing CODIS or *any* large database system from reaching its full potential.

The other factor that impeded the full development of CODIS was widespread concern about its possible misuses. Possibly the most contentious issue surrounding the development of a DNA database concerns who should be included. A number of possibilities exist, including:

1. Anyone who has been *convicted* of a violent crime, such as murder, rape, or aggravated assault;

2. Anyone who has been *charged* with, but not necessarily convicted of, such a crime;

3. Anyone who has been *accused* of, but not necessarily charged with or convicted of, such a crime; and

4. Anyone convicted, charged, or accused of a less violent crime, such as burglary, soliciting, or shoplifting.

Various governmental units have adopted various criteria in creating their own DNA databases. Almost without exception, individuals who have been convicted of a violent crime have had to surrender DNA samples for entry into a state or national DNA database. But less stringent criteria are also used. In 2003, for example, Prime Minister Tony Blair recommended that the United Kingdom's Criminal Justice Bill of 1994 be amended to allow police officers to take DNA samples from individuals *arrested* for crimes, whether they were later charged or convicted of such crimes. The amendment strengthened the hand of British police officers, who previously had been allowed to take DNA samples only after an individual had actually been *charged* with a crime. At the time the amendment was proposed, the United Kingdom already had a DNA database of more than 2 million samples, which translates into a rate of one out of every 30 citizens of the country having a DNA sample in the database. By comparison, there were about 1.3 million DNA samples in the U.S. CODIS, or about one sample for every 225 Americans.

A similar trend could be seen in the United States. In March 2003, President George W. Bush proposed that federal law be changed to require the collection of DNA samples from both juvenile offenders and adults who have been arrested but not convicted. The new policy would replace an existing practice of collecting DNA samples only from adults who had been convicted of certain violent crimes.

Proposals like those offered by Blair and Bush raise a host of problems for civil libertarians and for many ordinary citizens. What happens, for example, if a person is *arrested* for a crime but later found innocent of that crime? Will his or her DNA fingerprints then be removed from the DNA database? Those familiar with bureaucracies worry that such a correction may never occur and that the suspect will forever after retain this pseudo-criminal record.

Proponents and critics of DNA databases alike acknowledge their potential value in crime fighting. Probably the strongest argument in support of their use is the possibility of obtaining "cold hits" in solving a crime. The term *cold hit* is used to describe the situation in which DNA collected at the scene of a crime is matched against DNA from some individual whose DNA samples already reside in a DNA database. The first cold hit occurred in 1991 when evidence collected at a murder scene in Minneapolis, Minnesota, was matched with a DNA sample stored in the state's Bureau of Criminal Apprehension DNA database. The match allowed police to apprehend and charge a suspect named Martin Estrada Perez with the crime. Perez was later convicted of the murder, at least partially because of the DNA match.

As of the end of 2006, the federal DNA database, CODIS, contained more than 3.6 million profiles, had been responsible for more than 9,000 cold hits, and had assisted in more than 10,000 criminal investigations. Given these data, few people would argue about the potential value of DNA databases. But how serious are the problems involved in constructing such databases? At what point are the threats to civil liberties greater than the benefits obtained from increased conviction rates? As the efficiency of DNA-typing technologies increases and the temptation to construct DNA databases grows, such questions will continue to trouble research scientists, law enforcement officials, and concerned citizens.

Conclusion

Chemists have made a number of important contributions to forensic science over the past two centuries. When criminologists recognized the value of fingerprints as a reliable means of identifying individuals, they began to search for methods by which prints could be collected and interpreted. They drew on a number of chemical procedures—some already in existence and some invented for the purpose of fingerprint identification—to improve the use of fingerprinting as a forensic technique. Out of this research grew procedures such as the silver nitrate, iodine fuming, ninhydrin, and superglue tests and procedures such as small particle reagent analysis and vacuum metal deposition.

Chemists have also made valuable contributions to forensic serology, some dating to the mid-1800s. Schönbein's hydrogen peroxide test and van Deen's guaiac test were among the first chemical tests used in forensics, useful in identifying the presence of human blood at a crime scene. A century later, the discovery of isoenzymes and polymorphic proteins greatly expanded the procedures available for correlating blood samples with specific individuals. Forensic chemists have also extended the methods of blood testing for use with other bodily fluids, such as semen and saliva.

Chemical tests for drugs and poisons also have a long history. An important turning point in the history of forensic science, in fact, was the discovery of the first chemical test for a poison, the Marsh test, invented in 1832. Toxicology may be the single area of forensic science in which chemistry has made the greatest number of contributions. Today hundreds of specific chemical tests can identify a large array of drugs and poisons.

Some of the most impressive developments in forensic chemistry are related to tests for arson and explosives investigations. Given the devastation usually associated with such events, the ability of researchers to track chemicals used in the perpetration of such crimes is amazing. Forensic chemists today routinely reconstruct arson and explosives events relying on minute amounts of remnants.

For all of the progress made by forensic chemists, however, nothing quite matches the development of DNA typing as a method for identifying individuals. The procedure has an advantage over fingerprinting in that it rests on a certifiable and provable scientific basis. It also surpasses all other forensic tests in the degree of sensitivity, with the ability to identify individuals with a probability of one out of a million or better. Little wonder that most forensic scientists acknowledge that the gold standard of identification is likely to be DNA typing for the foreseeable future.

GLOSSARY

adsorption   The physical process by which atoms, molecules, or ions adhere to the surface of a solid or liquid.

alkaloids   A large class of naturally occurring compounds with complex structures that usually includes a heterocyclic nitrogen-containing ring. *See also* HETEROCYCLE.

allele   Any one of the two or more forms in which a gene may occur.

allelic ladder   In DNA typing, a term that refers to a set of DNA fragments of precise and known size that can be used to estimate the size of an unknown DNA fragment.

amplification   The process by which a single copy of DNA is reproduced many times over as a result of the polymerase chain reaction.

annealing   The step during a polymerase chain reaction in which a DNA primer is attached to a segment of DNA to be reproduced.

autorad   *See* AUTORADIOGRAPH.

autoradiograph   An X-ray photograph that shows marks produced radioactively or by means of chemiluminescence in the analysis of a DNA fragment.

base pair   Either of the two nitrogen base combinations (guanine and cytosine or thymine and adenine) that is found in a DNA molecule.

bifurcations   Regions of a fingerprint in which a ridge branches into two or more directions.

characterization   The process by which a sample of material is identified as belonging to some specific category.

cold hit   An event in which DNA collected at the scene of a crime is matched against DNA from some individual whose DNA sample already resides in a DNA database.

combustion   An oxidation reaction in which noticeable heat and light are produced.

confirmatory test   A test that is performed to authenticate some association between two variables with a high degree of probability. *See also* PRESUMPTIVE TEST.

criminalistics   The analysis, comparison, identification, and interpretation of evidence collected in a crime.

denaturation   The process by which the three-dimensional structure of a protein or nucleic acid molecule is destroyed by the addition of heat, chemicals, or some other agent. In DNA typing, the term refers specifically to the process by which a DNA molecule is uncoiled and/or separated into its two constituent strands.

DNA database   A large collection of DNA samples taken from individuals accused of, arrested for, charged with, and/or convicted of certain types of crimes.

DNA fingerprinting   *See* DNA TYPING.

DNA primer   *See* DNA PROBE.

DNA probe   A synthetically produced DNA fragment designed to match some specific DNA target. Also known as a DNA primer.

DNA profiling   *See* DNA TYPING.

DNA typing   A set of techniques used to compare two DNA samples, such as those taken from two individuals or one or more individuals and one or more pieces of evidence.

exothermic reaction   A chemical reaction in which heat is given off.

extension   The step during a polymerase chain reaction in which DNA polymerase enzymes add nucleotides to a segment of DNA specifically marked off by DNA primers.

false-negative   A test result that suggests that a particular substance is absent from a sample when it is actually present.

false-positive   A test result that suggests that a particular substance is present in a sample when it is really not.

fire triangle   A diagram commonly used to illustrate the three conditions needed for any fire: a fuel, an oxidizing agent, and heat.

flammable range   The concentrations of fuel and oxygen within which a fuel will burn.

flash point   The lowest temperature at which a liquid vaporizes sufficiently to permit combustion.

gas chromatography   An analytical technique for separating the components of a mixture based on their relative affinities for some material over which they are passed.

gene   A term originally invented to describe the unit of hereditary transmission of characteristics, now known to consist of a segment of a DNA molecule.

genetic marker   Any portion of a DNA molecule with a clearly defined genetic characteristic.

glowing combustion   Combustion that occurs rapidly enough to produce noticeable heat and light but not a visible flame.

grooves   Valley-like regions of a fingerprint or a ballistic marking.

heterocycle   An organic ring compound whose molecule structure contains some element other than carbon in its ring.

high-molecular-weight DNA   A DNA fragment with a size of at least 20,000 to 25,000 base pairs.

hydrocarbon detector   A device for detecting the presence of hydrocarbons.

identification   The determination of the chemical and physical properties of a substance with as much certainty as permitted by the tools and technology available.

ignition point   *See* IGNITION TEMPERATURE.

ignition temperature   The lowest temperature at which a substance will begin to burn and then continue to burn without the additional application of additional external heat.

individualization   The concept that any individual piece of evidence can be conclusively linked to a specific individual.

islands   Sections of a fingerprint in which ridges close in upon themselves.

junk DNA   Sections of a DNA molecule with no known function.

kindling point   *See* IGNITION TEMPERATURE.

ligase   An enzyme that catalyzes the formation of chemical bonds.

locus   The position of a gene on a chromosome.

loops   Closed segments in a fingerprint.

lyase   An enzyme that catalyzes the breaking of chemical bonds.

marker   *See* GENETIC MARKER.

minutiae   Ridges and grooves that make up a fingerprint pattern.

monomer   A small molecule that can join with other molecules to make large chains known as a polymer.

multiplexing   The process in the polymerase chain reaction by which more than one locus on a DNA molecule is analyzed at the same time.

nucleotide   A chemical compound consisting of the sugar deoxyribose, a phosphate group, and one of four nitrogen bases; the basic unit of a DNA molecule.

organic extraction   A procedure used in DNA typing for the separation of DNA from other contaminating materials.

oxidation-reduction reaction   A chemical reaction in which one chemical species loses one or more electrons to a second chemical species.

PCR   *See* POLYMERASE CHAIN REACTION.

polymer   A large molecule made up of many individual units (monomers) joined to each other.

polymerase   An enzyme that catalyzes the bonding of two groups to make a larger group.

polymerase chain reaction (PCR)   A method used in DNA typing that depends on the production of multiple copies of a relatively small fragment of DNA.

polymorphic   Existing in more than one form, as in the various alleles that a gene may possess.

power of discrimination   The ability of a test to distinguish between any two individuals, conditions, circumstances, or events chosen at random.

presumptive test   A test that is performed when there is some reasonable basis for believing that some positive result will be obtained. *See also* CONFIRMATORY TEST.

primary explosive   An explosive that is very sensitive and unstable and may be detonated easily by the application of heat, mechanical shock, or an electric spark.

pyrolyze   To cause the chemical decomposition of a material by applying extreme heat.

quantitation The process of determining how much of a material, such as DNA, is present in a sample.

rate of detonation The speed at which an expanding gas moves outward from the point of detonation after an explosion.

redox *See* OXIDATION-REDUCTION REACTION.

restriction enzyme An enzyme that cuts a DNA molecule in specific regions characterized by certain base-pair patterns.

restriction fragment length polymorphism (RFLP) A method of DNA typing that compares the lengths of specific sections of the DNA taken from two or more sources.

reverse dot-blot test A procedure for analyzing sequence polymorphisms in the polymerase chain reaction process.

ridges Elevated regions of a fingerprint, frequently referred to as friction ridges.

rifling The process by which spiral grooves are etched into the inner surface of a gun barrel.

secondary explosive An explosive that is more stable than a primary explosive and which, if ignited in open air, tends to burn quietly rather than exploding.

sequence-specific oligonucleotide test *See* REVERSE DOT-BLOT TEST.

serum The clear, liquid part of the blood that remains after blood cells and clotting proteins have been removed.

short tandem repeat (STR) Any tandem repeat with a relatively small number of repeating base pairs. *See also* TANDEM REPEAT.

slot-blot test A test commonly used for determining the amount of DNA present in a sample to be examined.

"sniffer" A device for detecting the presence of hydrocarbons.

Southern blot A procedure by which DNA segments are transferred from a gel electrophoresis platform to a sheet of nylon.

STR *See* SHORT TANDEM REPEAT.

taggant A tiny particle added to an explosive consisting of a number of layers of melamine plastic and used to identify the type of explosive and the point at which it was made.

tandem repeat Any section of a DNA molecule in which a particular pattern of base pairs appears more than once. *See also* SHORT TANDEM REPEAT.

FURTHER READING

PRINT RESOURCES

Almirall, Jose R., and Kenneth G. Furton. *Forensic Science Explained: Guide for Understanding the Use of Science.* Boca Raton, Fla.: CRC Press, 2005.

Bell, Suzanne. *The Facts On File Dictionary of Forensic Science.* New York: Facts On File, 2004.

Bertsch, Wolfgang. *Chemical Analysis for the Arson Investigator and Attorney.* Boca Raton, Fla.: CRC Press, 2005.

De Forest, Peter R., E. E. Gaensslen, and Henry C. Lee. *Forensic Science: An Introduction to Criminalistics.* New York: McGraw Hill, 1983.

Fuller, Charlie. *Forensic Science: Crime and Detection.* Broomall, Pa.: Mason Crest, 2004.

Inman, Keith, and Norah Rudin. *Principles and Practice of Criminalistics: The Profession of Forensic Science.* Boca Raton, Fla.: CRC Press, 2001.

Jones, Gary W. *Introduction to Fingerprint Comparison.* Temecula, Calif.: Staggs Publishing, 2000.

Levine, Barry, ed. *Principles of Forensic Toxicology.* 2nd ed. Washington, D.C.: AACC Press, 2003.

Liu, Ray H., and Daniel E. Gadzala. *Handbook of Drug Analysis: Applications in Forensic and Clinical Laboratories.* Washington, D.C.: American Chemical Society, 1997.

Maltoni, Davide. *Handbook of Fingerprint Recognition.* New York: Springer Verlag, 2003.

Rolih, Susan, and W. John Judd, eds. *Serological Methods in Forensic Science.* New York: American Association of Blood Banks, 1985.

Rudin, Norah, and Keith Inman. *An Introduction to Forensic DNA Analysis.* 2nd ed. Boca Raton, Fla.: CRC Press, 2002.

Saferstein, Richard. *Criminalistics: An Introduction to Forensic Science.* 7th ed. Upper Saddle River, N.J.: Prentice Hall, 2001.

Thorwald, Jürgen. *The Century of the Detective.* New York: Harcourt, Brace & World, 1964.

Tilstone, William J. *Forensic Science: An Encyclopedia of History, Methods, and Techniques.* Santa Barbara, Calif.: ABC-CLIO, 2004.

INTERNET RESOURCES

"Alan Barbour's Forensic Toxicology Links." Available online. URL: http://home.lightspeed.net/~abarbour/links.htm. Accessed on October 1, 2006.

Brief History of Forensic DNA Typing. Available online. URL: http://www.cstl.nist.gov/biotech/strbase/ppt/intro.pdf. Accessed on October 1, 2006.

Complete Latent Print Examination. Available online. URL: http://www.clpex.com. Accessed on October 1, 2006.

Criminal Justice Resources: Forensic Science. Available online. URL: http://www.lib.msu.edu/harris23/crimjust/forsci.htm. Last revised September 8, 2005.

Demonstrative Evidence. Available online. URL: http://faculty.ncwc.edu/toconnor/425/425lect03.htm. Last updated February 6, 2006.

Digital Fingerprints. Available online. URL: http://www.eneate.freeserve.co.uk. Last updated May 2005.

DNA Typing and Identification. Available online. URL: http://faculty.ncwc.edu/toconnor/425/425lect15.htm. Last updated February 6, 2006.

Forensic Serology. Available online. URL: http://faculty.ncwc.edu/toconnor/425/425lect13.htm. Last updated February 8, 2006.

Forensic Toxicology. Available online. URL: http://faculty.ncwc.edu/toconnor/425/425lect14.htm. Last updated February 8, 2006.

Latent Print Examination. Available online. URL: http://www.onin.com/fp. Accessed on October 1, 2006.

Rykerd, Charles L. *"Guide for the Selection of Commercial Explosives Detection Systems for Law Enforcement Applications,"* NIJ Guide 100-99, September 1999. Available online. URL: http://www.ncjrs.org/pdf-files1/nij/178913-1.pdf. Accessed on October 1, 2006.

Simplified Testing Procedure for the Major Drugs of Abuse. Available online. URL: http://www.bvda.com/EN/download/np_instructions_2002.pdf. Accessed on October 1, 2006.

The World Wide Web Virtual Library: Forensic Toxicology. Available online. URL: http://home.lightspeed.net/~abarbour/vlibft.html. Last updated February 13, 2005.

INDEX

DEMCO